ESSENTIAL HISTORIES

THE CHINESE CIVIL WAR 1945–49

Michael Lynch

OSPREY PUBLISHING
Bloomsbury Publishing Plc
Kemp House, Chawley Park, Cumnor Hill, Oxford OX2 9PH, UK
29 Earlsfort Terrace, Dublin 2, Ireland
1385 Broadway, 5th Floor, New York, NY 10018, USA
E-mail: info@ospreypublishing.com
www.ospreypublishing.com

OSPREY is a trademark of Osprey Publishing Ltd

First published in Great Britain in 2022

© Osprey Publishing Ltd, 2022

The text in this edition is revised and updated from: *ESS 61: The Chinese Civil War 1945–49* (Osprey Publishing, 2010).

A catalogue record for this book is available from the British Library.

ISBN: PB 9781472853141;
eBook 9781472853134;
ePDF 9781472853127;
XML 9781472853158

22 23 24 25 26   10 9 8 7 6 5 4 3 2 1

Cover, page design and layout by Stewart Larking
Maps by Peter Bull Art Studio, revised by J B Illustrations
Index by Zoe Ross
Printed and bound in India by Replika Press Private Ltd.

Osprey Publishing supports the Woodland Trust, the UK's leading woodland conservation charity.

To find out more about our authors and books visit www.ospreypublishing.com. Here you will find extracts, author interviews, details of forthcoming events and the option to sign up for our newsletter.

Dedication
For TOM LYNCH, born 2008.

Editor's notes
The following abbreviations are used throughout the text:
CCP – Chinese Communist Party (the Reds)
GMD – Guomindang (the Nationalists)
NRA – Nationalist Revolutionary Army (renamed the Republic of China Army in 1946)
PLA – People's Liberation Army (originally the Red Army)
PRC – People's Republic of China (Communist China)

Many Chinese persons and places have alternative forms to their name. This book uses the most modern or the most familiar form. To avoid confusion, the first time a name is cited it will be followed by its alternative in parenthesis, e.g., Beijing (Peking), Chiang Kai-shek (Jiang Jieshi).

CONTENTS

INTRODUCTION

The Chinese Civil War of 1946–49, one of the bloodiest conflicts of the 20th century, took the lives of over five million soldiers and civilians. It was not a new struggle but the latest stage in a conflict that went back two decades. It was fought between two parties, the Guomindang (GMD or Nationalists) and the Chinese Communist Party (CCP or Reds), both of whom claimed sovereignty over the land and people of the whole of China.

To understand how that situation came about it is necessary to go back to at least 1911. It was in that year that the centuries-old imperial system, which had seen China ruled by successive royal dynasties, such as the Han and the Ming, collapsed. In October 1911, what proved to be the last dynasty, the Qing (Manchu), was unable to prevent China's domination and humiliation by the Western powers and by its neighbour Japan, and was faced with a mutiny among its own forces, which it could not control. Drained of real authority and self-belief, the Qing chose not to fight on but to abdicate. This was the first of China's modern revolutions. To replace the fallen imperial system a Republic was established, but from the first the new regime was too weak to create stability. In effect, central government no longer operated. China fractured into a series of regions dominated by locally powerful military commanders, known as warlords, who became a law unto themselves. The turmoil led to the separate development of the two revolutionary parties, the GMD and the CCP, both committed to the idea that China could not be regenerated as a nation unless the warlords were crushed.

This shared aim led initially to military co-operation between the two parties. They came together in a United Front which by 1927 had largely achieved its objective of suppressing the warlords. However, at that point, the

GMD leader, Chiang Kai-shek (Jiang Jieshi), possessed of a visceral hatred of Communism, turned against his former ally the CCP and attempted to destroy it totally. He was prevented from doing so only by the desperate flight of the Communists in the mid-1930s from their beleaguered southern base to a northern province where they set up the Yanan soviet with Mao Zedong (Mao Tse-tung) as its dominant leader.

A complicating factor in the bitter GMD–CCP relations was the presence in China of occupying Japanese forces. Beginning in 1931 with its invasion of Manchuria, Japan went on to launch a full-scale occupation of China in 1937. Since both parties were formally resolved to resist the Japanese, they came together intermittently in a series of united fronts against the enemy. Yet this did not betoken genuine agreement between then and they continued to fight each other even while warring against Japan. The reality was that there were two conflicts going on in China after 1937: the struggle against Japan and what amounted to a Nationalist-Communist intermittent civil war. So it was, therefore, that when Japan was finally defeated in 1945, Chinese internal conflicts remained unresolved. Further conflict loomed.

The disposition of the two sides when their war was renewed in 1946 had been determined a year earlier by the manner in which World War II ended in the East. The Japanese surrender in August 1945 had marked an apparent pinnacle of success for Chiang Kai-shek, who, as Nationalist leader, had governed the Republic of China since 1936. He now emerged from the Pacific War as a world statesman. Yet, welcome as victory was for Chiang, the way it had come about was tinged with disappointment for him.

His hope had been that the defeat of the Japanese would also see the defeat of the Chinese Communists, who, under Mao Zedong, aimed ultimately to take power from the GMD. Chiang had expected that the final stages of the war against Japan would climax with a massive landing of American troops on the Chinese mainland,

OPPOSITE
Sun Yatsen (seated) and Chiang Kai-shek in 1925. Sun was China's first great modern revolutionary, whose 'Three People's Principles' – nationalism, socialism and democracy – were an inspiration to both Chiang Kai-shek and Mao Zedong. (Photo by DE AGOSTINI PICTURE LIBRARY/ Getty Images)

who would eventually overwhelm the Japanese. In the process they would drive the Communists from their bases in northern China, leaving Chiang and the Nationalists as the undisputed masters of the nation.

But it did not work out as Chiang Kai-shek had planned. The Pacific conflict ended not with the crushing of the Japanese forces in a bloody, attritional conflict in China, but with the atomic bombing of Japan itself. It was the nuclear devastation of Hiroshima and Nagasaki with the loss of 150,000 lives in August 1945 that persuaded the Japanese to surrender unconditionally. This sudden and dramatic close to the war meant the cancellation of the plans for the large-scale movement of American forces to China, and thus undermined Chiang Kai-shek's internal strategy.

Nor was it merely that the Communists remained undefeated. The abrupt ending of the war directly enhanced their position. The Japanese commanders in China chose to make their formal surrenders to the nearest Chinese military authority. Since in a number of areas this meant the local Communist commander, the CCP found themselves being treated as the proper representatives of the Republic of China. Chiang appealed to his US ally to rush his troops to positions where they could take the local Japanese surrenders. The Americans responded by organizing a major airlift to the northern areas, but it proved only partially successful. The Communists were strong enough to continue asserting their authority over the 'liberated areas' – their term for those parts of China that they had controlled or taken since the 1930s.

Chiang's problems did not end there. A further restriction on the Nationalists' supremacy was the presence in Manchuria, China's most northerly region, of a large Soviet army. In keeping with a long-term promise made at the Yalta Conference in February 1945, the USSR had joined the war against Japan three days after the Hiroshima bombing. On the pretext of freeing Manchuria from Japanese control, the Soviet forces had taken over the region for their own ends. They were to stay there until March 1946, leaving only after they had stripped the region of over $2 billion worth of plant and machinery.

Chiang Kai-shek, however, had little ground for formal complaint. Only days after the Soviet troops crossed into Manchuria, his Nationalist government had signed a Sino-Soviet Treaty of Friendship, which accepted the USSR's right to enter China. Chiang's willingness to make this concession was explained by his political aim. He was prepared to allow Soviet forces into Manchuria on the understanding that the USSR confirmed its recognition of his party as the only legitimate authority in China. Chiang also calculated that the Soviet forces might well be able to achieve what he had originally hoped the Americans would do – destroy the Communists.

What made this a realistic expectation was that Joseph Stalin, the Soviet leader, was far from being wholly supportive of the Chinese Communists. From the time of the CCP's formation in the 1920s, Stalin had consistently judged that it was not strong enough to survive in China. Moreover, he did not want an outright Communist victory in China. As late as 1949, Stalin was urging Mao to accept a compromise peace with the Nationalists. His motives were national and personal as well as political. He was unhappy at the prospect of a strong China on the USSR's Asian borders and feared that if Mao were to become the all-powerful leader of China this would make him a formidable international rival.

It was also the case that the USA was initially far from antagonistic towards the Chinese Communists. It had seen them as vital allies in the struggle against Japan. It was thus with the best of intentions that the Americans sought to lessen the strife in post-war China by bringing the CCP and the GMD together in a compromise settlement. It was under American auspices that, in August 1945, Chiang and Mao Zedong met personally for the first time in 20 years. The two leaders agreed on a truce, but it is doubtful whether either of them intended it to last. The differences between them ran too deep.

LEFT
Mao Zedong in 1937 (aged 44) in Yanan. It was during his years here that Mao developed the ruthless political and military strategies that would eventually take him to power. (Universal History Archive/ Getty Images)

It was no surprise, therefore, that within a few months such agreement as had been reached had broken down. Formal negotiations did continue, but by June 1946 the two sides were openly fighting each other again. The Americans – who had previously not fully grasped the depth of the GMD–CCP animosity – abandoned their role as mediators and by January 1947 had withdrawn from China, although they continued to provide the GMD with military advisers and equipment.

OPPOSITE
A young Chiang Kai-shek as a cadet in Whampoa in the early 1920s. (Photo by: Carl Simon/ United Archives/ Universal Images Group via Getty Images)

The war was often a complex affair at local level. The lines between Communists and Nationalists were often blurred by the interplay of local activists. In some areas, villages formed armed units to protect themselves against the forces of both sides. To increase their security, these self-protection units often did deals with local bandits and marauders. In other regions, resistance groups, which had first been formed to fight the Japanese, did not disband after Japan's surrender but stayed together as a local army. Unsophisticated peasants did not find it easy to distinguish between Nationalists, Communists, and armed marauders. In their experience, the soldiers – whatever their uniform or allegiance – were equally likely to steal from, beat, rape or murder them. It is important to acknowledge that the peasantry seldom had a strong sense of China as a nation that was directly relevant to them. The peasants' experience was local; they lived their lives locally, and it was that locality that defined their opportunities. Indeed, it was this very localism that Mao and Chiang in their different ways were trying to break down and replace with a sense of identity on a national scale.

The Nationalists, after some seemingly impressive successes in the first year of the war, when they attempted to drive the Communists from their northern bases, were unable to achieve a single major victory between 1947 and 1949. By 1949 their grip on northern, central and southern China had been broken in a series of victorious People's Liberation Army (PLA) campaigns. In October 1949, in the restored capital, Beijing (Peking), Mao Zedong claimed that a new nation had been created, the People's Republic of China (PRC), in which the CCP was the sovereign power. Chiang, knowing that the position was irrecoverable and to avoid having to surrender, abandoned the mainland. In December, he fled with the remnants of his forces to the island of Taiwan. There he established a separate Nationalist state, which, in defiance of the Communists, claimed to be the legitimate government of the whole of China.

OPPOSITE
Nationalist soldiers on the march in 1945. Within months of the Japanese surrender in August, Chiang's forces would be fighting the Communists. (Photo by Paul Popper/Popperfoto via Getty Images)

WARRING SIDES

Nationalists and Communists

The Guomindang had come into being in the first decade of the 20th century with the aim of modernizing China. Under its founder, Sun Yatsen, the GMD had advanced a revolutionary programme whose first objective was to bring down the ruling Qing dynasty. Yet, despite its contribution to the Chinese Revolution of 1911, which brought an end to the Qing, the GMD did not control the Chinese Republic that was then established. Central authority remained weak and the Nationalists, whose power base was in the south of China, were unable to control affairs. Government was carried on by President Yuan Shikai, a reactionary general of the old imperial army. By the time of his death in 1916, China was in a worse state than it had been in under the Qing. Near bankrupt, it had to rely heavily on a foreign financial consortium led by Japan, its neighbour and traditional enemy.

China's weakness in relation to Japan was further exposed in the aftermath of World War I. In the hope that by contributing to the Western Allies' war effort it would gain recognition of its rights, China had declared war on Germany in 1917. However, in the Versailles peace settlement of 1919, Chinese claims were simply ignored. Having had its soldiers disdainfully treated during the war as mere 'coolies', fit only for back-breaking labour behind the lines, China was brusquely informed at Versailles that it would not have its territories restored; the Chinese provinces formerly occupied by Germany were to be transferred to Japan. The news from Versailles created ferment in China. Outraged students took to the streets in protest against the humiliation of their nation and the failure of the Republican government to resist. Their actions were the beginning of a sustained reaction, known from its starting date as the May Fourth Movement. Inspired by an intense nationalism, the movement called on all Chinese citizens to restore their nation's former independence and greatness by ridding China of foreign domination.

It was in the atmosphere created by May Fourth that a new radical party was born. In Shanghai in 1921, the Chinese Communist Party came into being. One of the CCP's founder members was Mao Zedong, a 28-year-old peasant from Hunan province. What had turned Mao into a Marxist was not abstract theory; he had been a revolutionary before he was a Marxist. Angered by the failure of the Republic to fulfil the hopes placed in it, and ashamed of his people's continuing subjection to foreign control, he had been searching for a political path that China could follow to achieve its freedom. Influenced by the 1917 Bolshevik Revolution in Russia, which he saw as the overthrow of imperialism by the Russian people, he believed that Marxism provided the programme he had been seeking.

The Comintern, the Soviet agency for developing international revolution, had been involved in the formation of the Chinese Communist Party in 1921. It tried thereafter to direct the CCP's policy. Mao, however, never allowed himself to be overawed by the USSR, despite its claim as senior partner to be entitled to instruct the Chinese in revolutionary strategy. His successful resistance to Soviet encroachment was most evident in his victories in the 1920s and 1930s over a series of party rivals whom the Soviet Union tried to impose on the CCP. It was because all Chinese revolutionaries shared the same basic ambition as Sun

Chiang's wife, Soong Meiling (seated), and her sisters Ailing (to Meiling's right) and Qingling (edge of picture). The Soong sisters were Nationlist celebrities. Chiang believed they projected an appealing image of the GMD. (Photo by Hulton Archive/ Getty Images)

Yatsen's Nationalists – the defeat of China's external and internal enemies – that the CCP and GMD, in the early stages, were not rivals but partners. Indeed, many revolutionaries, including Mao, belonged to both. The fellow feeling between the parties was stimulated by their joint wish to destroy the warlords – the term for those military leaders who, since 1912, had seized upon the weakness of the central Republican government to set themselves up as independent rulers in China's provinces. It was in order to crush the warlords that the GMD and the CCP formed a United Front in 1924. Over the next three years their combined armies proved increasingly successful and by 1927 the warlords had been largely overcome.

The year 1927 was critical in China's political development. It was in that year that Chiang Kai-shek, judging that the United Front had served its purpose in breaking the warlords, turned on his Communist allies in an attempt to annihilate them. Chiang's violent move, known as 'the White Terror', was a product of his hatred of Communism. Since fighting his way to the leadership of the GMD in the power struggle that followed the death of Sun Yatsen in 1925, his primary concern had been to crush his internal enemies – the Communists. Chiang had gone to the USSR in the early 1920s to be trained as a revolutionary, but his experience there, rather than drawing him to Communism, did the opposite. He returned to China with an abiding detestation of Marxism, which became the motif of his political career. It remained his conviction that China could not progress towards true modernity unless it first destroyed Mao's Communists.

Consequently, over the next ten years Chiang devoted himself to hunting the CCP to extinction. He very nearly succeeded. In a series of encirclement campaigns, he tightened the ring around the Communist bases in southern China. Chiang's chief military adviser in these campaigns was a German general, Hans von Seeckt, whose presence in China between 1934 and 1935, as part of a German military mission, was evidence of the close links between the Nationalists and Hitler's Third Reich. It was Seeckt who drew up plans for reforming Chiang's army into 60 highly trained divisions. Although only a third of these had been created by the time of the Japanese invasion in 1937, Seeckt's influence had been an important one. The Nationalists' tactics, discipline and uniforms were all based on German models and it was Nazi Germany that, until 1936, supplied most of the GMD's weaponry.

By 1934, such was the build-up of pressure on the Communists' main base in Jiangxi in southern China that it was only by a desperate flight that Mao's Communists survived. It was their escape from Jiangxi to Yanan, in the northern province of Shaanxi, that became

enshrined in Communist legend as the Long March of 1934–35. This was portrayed as a 6,000-mile odyssey, whose survivors, having come through the most extreme hazards, had been forged into an irresistible historical force, one destined to rule China. Much of this was hyperbole, and in fact the march had begun as a rout. Yet there was no denying that the CCP had successfully defied the Nationalists. Chiang would continue to attack the Communists, but events were to show that his last opportunity to destroy them had passed.

One of the most significant outcomes of the Long March was the consolidation of Mao's position as leader of the CCP. Once established in Yanan in 1935, Mao set about constructing a Communist soviet that over the next decade came to rival Chiang's Nationalist government. That Mao was able to do so was largely explained by a factor that dominated Chinese politics until 1945 – the occupation of China by Japan. In 1931, as a first step towards a massive expansion into Asia, Japan had occupied the northern region of Manchuria, renamed it Manchuguo (Manchukuo) and installed a puppet regime there. From this base, the Japanese forces began to spread out into neighbouring regions.

Dedicated defender of his nation though he was, Chiang Kai-shek seemed slow to respond to the Japanese action; his primary aim was still to crush the Communists. The CCP made capital out of this by asserting that they, not the Nationalists, were the true champions of China. Then a dramatic development in 1936 enabled them to seize the initiative. One of Chiang's own generals, unhappy with his leader's apparent lack of zeal in resisting the Japanese, led a mutiny that resulted in Chiang being taken prisoner at Xian. He was then handed over to the Communists, who, instead of killing him as he at first expected, offered him a deal. In return for his calling off the campaigns against them, they were prepared not merely to release him but to work under his military leadership in a renewal of the GMD–CCP alliance, this time directed against the Japanese. Chiang's predicament gave him no choice but to accept the terms

OPPOSITE
Hans von Seeckt helped create the basis for a modern Nationalist army and air force. Arguably, had his encirclement strategy been consistently followed in the 1930s, Mao and the CCP would have been totally destroyed. (Photo by Miller /Topical Press Agency/Getty Images)

offered. The curious result of this Xian Incident was, therefore, that in December 1936 he became recognized as the leader of the nation by the Communists he had been trying to destroy.

The clemency shown by the CCP towards Chiang was not sympathy but expediency. In exchange for sparing him, they had obtained recognition of their own legitimacy. None of this, however, betokened a real understanding between the two parties. Their animosity remained. What tended to hide the true situation was the threat of Japan. Having established itself in Manchuria since 1931, Japan launched a full-scale invasion of China in 1937. Over the next eight years it occupied a third of the Chinese mainland, including China's most prosperous central states. One consequence of the occupation was the ending of the co-operation between Chiang and Nazi Germany. Hitler's growing friendship with Japan meant that the Nationalists could no longer call on German assistance in their struggle against the Japanese occupiers.

The post-Xian co-operation between the CCP and the Nationalists was always a strained affair and by 1940 fighting between them had broken out again. Thus between 1940 and 1945 there were two wars going on in China: the national war of resistance against the Japanese and the continuing CCP–GMD Civil War. To this could be added a third internal struggle – both Mao and Chiang were involved in asserting their authority within their own parties. Mao faced a number of leadership challenges during the Yanan period from 1935 to 1945, but none of these seriously threatened his dominance. Using the most ruthless means to crush internal opposition, he was by the early 1940s the undoubted master of the CCP. Chiang Kai-shek was never entirely master of his party in the way that Mao was of his. Nevertheless, Chiang's reputation soared once World War II spread to the Asian theatres. The Japanese attack on the American base at Pearl Harbor in December 1941 brought the USA into the war as an ally of China and elevated Chiang to the status of international statesman.

Yet not all the advantages were with the Nationalists. As enemies of Japan, the Chinese Communists were also the USA's allies. In time of war, the ideological differences between the capitalist Americans and Mao's Marxists took second place to the common aim of defeating the Japanese. Mao wanted help from the Soviet Union in his struggle with the Nationalists, but he was also aware that the USA was not necessarily hostile to him and his party. That was why in his dealings with the Americans he played down his hard-line Marxism and projected the idea that the Chinese Communists were essentially land reformers

This Communist poster, from the 1920s, continued to be used during the Civil War. It urges peasants, workers, and soldiers to fight against China's enemies, the imperialists and the warlords, and was extended after 1945 to include the GMD. (Library of Congress)

An example of Nationalist propaganda, showing a traditional Chinese hero overcoming the devil of Communism. (Library of Congress)

intent on improving the living conditions of China's rural poor. At the end of the war the Americans were assured by Stalin that the CCP were merely 'margarine' Communists and that the Soviet Union had no binding links with them. This encouraged the USA to believe that it could establish democracy in China by bringing the two sides together without interference from the USSR.

It was this conviction that inspired a series of US missions to China in the final year of the Pacific War. Both

Chiang and Mao were willing to play along with this, since both wanted continued US diplomatic recognition and material supplies. Some American advisers, taken in by the accommodating manner adopted by the Chinese Communists, even appealed to the State Department to abandon Chiang and give its full support to Mao. The USA later admitted that it had 'lost' China during this period. Despite its undoubted goodwill and good faith, it had misunderstood the nature of internal politics in China. In the brief period after the end of the war in 1945, before their relations hardened into a Cold War, there was a possibility that the Soviet Union and the USA might have reached an accommodation over China. But, as their behaviour during the years of the Chinese Civil War was to show, neither of the two great powers had fully grasped the reality of the situation.

Chiang Kai-shek, Roosevelt and Churchill in 1943; by the end of the Pacific War two years later, Chiang was at the high point of his renown as China's leader. (Bettmann/Getty Images)

As they stood in 1945 at the end of the Japanese war, Chiang's Nationalists seemed to hold the advantage. Better armed, possessing far larger armies and in control of the key strategic areas of China, the Nationalists looked set to triumph over the CCP. The Chinese Communists were restricted to bases in rural areas of northern China, and they had yet to make any real impact on the towns and cities. Yet, though this was a limitation, it was not as great a one as it first appeared. The Chinese were overwhelmingly a rural people; 90 per cent of the population were peasants, most of them eking out life at subsistence level. Both the Communist and Nationalist armies that faced each other were peasant armies, recruited mainly through coercion. This was particularly the case with the Nationalists, whose forces were largely conscripts. While not all the Communist troops were eager volunteers, a far higher proportion of the PLA's soldiers had enlisted willingly. The Civil War was to be a test of which side would prove more adept at turning its peasant forces into effective fighting units.

The NRA, 1945–49

In 1945 Chiang's Nationalist Revolutionary Army (NRA) was composed of around three million pressed and recruited troops. These were formed into 160 separate armies, each made up of three divisions, with a division varying between 5,000 and 10,000 troops. The divisions were sub-divided into brigades, regiments, battalions, companies and platoons. The army was never as organized as these bald figures might suggest. Indeed, it was lack of organization, especially in regard to the supply of essential ammunition and food, that was a constant problem for the NRA.

Chiang's military aim was to be head of an integrated national army that would respond to his every order. It was an objective he never fully achieved. Throughout the Civil War his armies were a mixed bunch. There were crack units that were devoted to him personally,

but too often his forces were a ragbag collection of units, committed only to their region and unwilling to take risks. Chiang's power to control them was always limited by the degree to which the local commanders were loyal to him. He was engaged in a continual effort to placate and persuade his army leaders, and his authority was always dependent upon deals being struck with local leaders. Chiang was seldom the master of the situation.

The officers in the NRA were of two main types. There were the fully trained men who had graduated from Nationalist military schools, such as Chiang's own elite Whampoa Academy, situated in Nanjing (Nanking), and Chengdu (Chengtu). Many of these had seen service during the Japanese war and had experience and ability. However, they were outnumbered by the second type: locally recruited officers who used bribes or influence to gain commissions, which they saw as a source of income. The commands they most coveted were those concerned with handling supplies and resources. Corruption became endemic among such officers, few of whom had relevant military training or experience. The hunger and brutality experienced by the rank-and-file recruits was often a consequence of their being at the mercy of this type of officer. Given the venality and the self-serving character of these officers, it followed that they were unenthusiastic warriors. They avoided contact with the enemy whenever possible and if engaged in battle were the first to surrender or defect when the going got tough.

Chiang's greatest problem in maintaining his armies as efficient fighting units was the high level of desertions. This had been a difficulty throughout Chinese military history. China was a vast country and the great majority of the population lived restricted lives. Life was local. Troops dreaded moving far away from their homes. When campaigns were protracted or took place in distant regions, peasant soldiers invariably grew homesick. The problem was worsened by the fact that the majority of the NRA's troops were conscripts, pressed into service

by ferocious recruiting squads who raided villages and dragged off the menfolk. In 1947, Chiang's government issued a General Mobilization decree giving it unlimited authority to conscript.

Although the punishments for desertion were ferocious, many still attempted it and the result was that Nationalist units were often decimated. It was not uncommon for NRA units to lose as much as one-tenth of their troop numbers per month through desertion. To prevent this, NRA officers resorted to roping their men together in groups of a dozen or so. Sometimes chains

Nationalist conscripts roped together. Enforced recruitment continued throughout the Civil War, and was a major reason for the Nationalists' unpopularity. (Library of Congress)

were used on those thought most likely to abscond. Units even marched tied together, giving the appearance of prisoners rather than soldiers. Troops were allowed to relieve themselves only at prescribed times and it had to be done en masse. At night or at rest, the bonds remained on.

The NRA became notorious for the brutal way it treated its ordinary soldiers. Forty per cent of conscripts deserted during basic training and another 20 per cent died from starvation. The International Red Cross calculated that in the periods of the Japanese occupation and civil wars from 1937 to 1949 over five million of those drafted into the Nationalist armies died. A system of individual responsibility was imposed, which required that each soldier keep watch over the next man behind or in front of him in the line; should he fail to stop that man from making off, he was punished by beatings and denial of rations. In general, it was shortage of food that caused the greatest suffering among the troops. Men in the ranks were constantly hungry. This was not necessarily because food supplies to the army broke down. Although this did frequently happen, the primary reason was the common practice among the officers of making money by selling army rations to crooked civilian rice or grain merchants. Troops were often reduced to surviving off compressed rice cakes, which they carried in their pockets and nibbled over a number of days.

Unsurprisingly, Nationalist morale declined. Feelings of homesickness and disorientation, an ever-present condition among peasant soldiers when campaigning far from their homes, gnawed at the Nationalist armies. A report in May 1947 from a high-ranking American diplomat in Shenyang contrasted the 'fighting spirit of the Communists with the exhaustion of the Nationalists and their growing indignation over disparity between officers' enrichment and soldiers' low pay, life, and their lack of interest in fighting far from home'.

When men are treated violently, they behave violently. What added to the brutality that conditioned army life

OPPOSITE
A Nationalist teenage soldier in Shanxi (Shansi) in 1947. (Philip Jowett)

was that the NRA ranks were also swollen by troops from the former warlord armies. These soldiers had invariably taken part in or witnessed the myriad and fearsome crimes associated with the unfettered use of warlord authority. Looting, rape, torture, execution and the burning of villages were the usual, not the exceptional, behaviour of such forces. The violence may not have been as systematically organized as that perpetrated by the Japanese occupiers, but it was something to which many areas of China had become accustomed by the 1940s. The terror in Sichuan province was described by one observer: 'The poor people suffer the scourge of militarism, more destructive than floods, more destructive than savage beasts. We must have soldiers, people say, so that the country will be strong. And the people become poorer and poorer! Where an army has passed, nothing grows but brambles.'

Despite the problems surrounding recruitment, the NRA's three million troops at the start of the war outnumbered the PLA by over three to one. This, and the wider range of territory they occupied, seemed to indicate that the Nationalists had a powerful advantage. But appearances were misleading. Chiang's forces were too thinly spread for an effective supply system to be maintained, and there was the added problem that the further from the command centre the forces were, the more difficult they were to control.

Chiang enjoyed very committed support from his general staff at headquarters. Indeed, his top commanders venerated him and rejoiced in regarding him as the 'Generalissimo'. But the downside of this was that they tended to vie with each other for his favour. Additionally, since they waited upon his word rather than using their own initiative when making decisions, this limited their independence and speed of action. Moreover, in competing for his approval they necessarily made it more difficult to co-operate among themselves. This created a particular problem in relation to the struggle for supplies. Individual generals would approach Chiang claiming that their particular needs gave them priority in the allocation of supplies and reserves. If he accepted their case, he would authorize their call for resources.

In order for a general to get his way, he needed to be able to approach Chiang directly. If the Generalissimo backed the idea put to him, it carried an authority that was then difficult for other military leaders to challenge. This, however, worked only at the top level. Lower down the chain of command, there was no guarantee that central directives would be obeyed if they ran counter to the interests of local commanders. Chiang often fumed over the manner in which strategic decisions made centrally were not followed in the field.

The PLA

There was a sense in which warlordism returned to China after the defeat of Japan. Contradicting Chiang's assertion that the Nationalist government was back in control, bandit gangs roamed many parts of the countryside. Owing allegiance to no one but themselves, they terrorized the areas in which they operated. Part of the appeal of the Communists was that in those areas where they met and crushed these gangs, their victories brought the ordinary peasants a respite from their miseries. Two consequences tended to follow. Impressed by the help given to them by the Communists, men in the villages joined the local PLA units. Recruits also came from among the defeated or captured bandits who threw in their lot with Mao's forces. In the latter case, it was seldom a matter of eager volunteers converting to the Communist cause; the new recruits knew that the alternative to joining up was to be shot. This is not to deny that in many instances they subsequently became committed CCP fighters, but the PLA could certainly be as unscrupulous as the NRA in the methods used to maintain its troop numbers.

In certain respects, Mao's armies were initially not well prepared for a civil war. One problem was that the Communist troops were not conditioned for a

sustained struggle. Their engagements with the Japanese had seldom been prolonged affairs; they were used to skirmishes, not pitched battles. As local volunteers or conscripts, most of the soldiers were unhappy once they left their own areas. One of their marching songs before 1945 had been 'Let's beat the Japanese, so we can all go home'. Officers often resorted to lying or deception to hide their real destination from the troops. When, for example, some southern CCP units were sent by troopship from Shandong province to Manchuria, they were told they were sailing to somewhere nearer home.

A further problem was the Communists' limited technical know-how. Despite the large number of weapons they had captured from the Japanese at the end of the Pacific War in 1945, including 700 tanks, 900 aircraft, 800,000 rifles, 14,000 machine guns and a large assortment of mortars, armoured vehicles and patrol boats, the PLA troops initially lacked a basic understanding of how to use them. This was especially true of the tanks and planes, which in the early stages of the war stood idle simply because the PLA lacked the knowledge of how to work and maintain them. It was only after Nationalist troops with technical expertise had defected from Chiang's army to Mao's that the PLA was able to employ the weapons effectively.

A major factor in the build-up of the PLA was the incorporation into the Communist ranks of the 200,000-strong Manchuguo army, made up of Chinese soldiers who had fought for Japan in Manchuria before 1945. Troops who refused to accept incorporation were 'cleansed' – a euphemism for executed. During the Civil War this was the fate that befell many PLA soldiers regarded as suspect by their Communist superiors. As many as 150,000 soldiers were 'cleansed' in this way, often after they had been tortured to make them reveal their associates.

PLA strength was also increased by the thousands of Japanese POWs who agreed under pressure to join the Communists; they acted as invaluable instructors in weapon use and tactics. By the end of the Civil War,

OPPOSITE TOP
PLA troops on parade showing the disciplined preparation and training for which they became renowned among their supporters and feared by their opponents. (Photo by Archiv Gerstenberg/ullstein bild via Getty Images)

OPPOSITE BOTTOM
PLA assault troops on the march during the successful attack in May 1949 on Shanghai, whose loss by the Nationalists was a decisive event in the Communists' eventual victory in the Civil War. (Photo by Keystone/Hulton Archive/Getty Images)

hundreds had lost their lives fighting for the Communist cause. North Korea, which fell under Soviet control at the end of the Pacific War, also contributed markedly to the war effort. Its proximity to the Communist bases in northern China made it a safe haven for PLA forces when they came under pressure. Moreover some 35,000 North Koreans fought in the Communist ranks, while others played a valuable role as civilian workers maintaining roads and railway lines in Communist-held areas.

At the time of the renewal of the Civil War in 1946, Mao defined the strategy his commanders were to follow: 'For defeating Chiang Kai-shek the general method of fighting is mobile warfare. Therefore, the abandonment of certain places or cities is not only unavoidable but also necessary.' This was a continuation of the guerrilla warfare that the Communists had successfully conducted against both the Nationalists and the Japanese. However, as events were to show, Mao intended this as only a temporary strategy. His ultimate aim was to turn the PLA into a modern fighting force that would eventually be able to fight on its own terms and be capable of defeating the Nationalists in open battle. What gave Mao confidence was that he had perceived the basic weakness of the enemy. He judged that while Chiang Kai-shek could call on American aid, 'the feelings of the people are against him, the morale of his troops is low, and his economy is in difficulty'.

Partly as a result of Maoist propaganda, the notion has developed that there had been a peasant revolution in the countryside during the Civil War. The claim is that, beginning with the Manchurian peasants, the rural peoples of China rejected the Nationalists and appealed to the Communists to set up a new political and social order. This is largely myth. The CCP certainly gained from the general resentment against Chiang's GMD government and its excesses, but it is not true that the Communists enjoyed mass popular support. The creation of what the CCP called 'liberated' areas over which they held sway was far more often than not a consequence of Communist forces imposing themselves on those areas. 'Liberation' was enforced on local peoples, not chosen by them.

When the Communists came to write the history of their coming to power, they naturally portrayed it as a spontaneous rising of the people, who turned to Mao and the Red Army for deliverance from the depredations of local bandits, the misery of landlord oppression and the brutalities of the Nationalists. But the reality was often quite different. A grim feature of the Civil War was the severe, often savage, way in which the Communists imposed their authority in the liberated areas. In the years 1945–49, over one million landlords were killed, their deaths usually coming after they had been subjected to the most brutal treatment. That some of the local peasants eagerly joined in with the terrorizing of the landlords was more a matter of satisfying long-standing local grievances than an embracing of Communism.

Although the Communists boasted of their practice of giving peasants in the liberated areas political representation by setting up village committees, the fact was that every committee had to have a CCP member on it with the power to veto decisions and direct policy. Moreover, the CCP was quite prepared to abandon the people of the liberated areas when the Nationalist threat became too great. There are no instances of the Communists putting themselves at risk of defeat by the GMD in order to defend the liberated areas. The calculation was always military, never humanitarian.

Yet it is not difficult to understand why so many of the localities were prepared, at least initially, to support the Communists' land campaigns. The warlords and the Japanese occupiers had shown scant regard for the traditional patterns of life on the land, and the miseries of the peasants had increased. The landlords had hardly enhanced their reputation during the years of Japanese occupation. Many of them had collaborated, but simply assumed that with the ending of the war in 1945 they were entitled, along with those landlords who had been ousted during the occupation, to return to their property and their privileges. They had learned nothing and forgotten nothing.

The result was that any party able to convince the peasants that it genuinely cared for them was likely to win support. Despite its promise to give priority to land reform and the ending of poverty, Chiang's government by the late 1940s could hardly claim success in this area. Indeed, one of the most unpopular steps that it took was to give military backing to those landlords who were prevented by local resistors from returning to their former properties or who had been dispossessed since they had returned. This provided an opportunity for the CCP to win over the peasantry. Aware that the peasants would be very willing to identify landlord greed as the chief cause of their suffering, the Communists engaged in the ritual public humiliation of landowners. It was invariably a brutal business, with the peasants being urged to vent their fury and frustration on their exploiters.

Huang Chin-Chi, a landlord, pinioned and forced to kneel on sharp stones, faces a people's court in a Communist liberated area. Such scenes often climaxed with the public denunciation, beating and killing of the accused. (Bettmann/Getty Images)

The attack upon the landlords was the prelude to a series of struggle sessions that provided the means for the Communists to control the countryside. Peasants were required to hold regular public gatherings, at which those judged sympathetic to the landlords were forced to confess and accept punishment. These struggle sessions soon deteriorated into occasions for the peasants to settle old scores and feuds. If enough villagers ganged up on an unpopular individual or family, the accusations themselves were taken as proof of guilt. The screaming, shouting and chanting that accompanied these 'people's trials' generated the type of hysteria associated with extreme religious rituals.

Such was the emotional intensity of these gatherings that Mao used them as a way of indoctrinating the soldiers in the PLA. Recruits were encouraged to join in the bitter attacks on the landlords for their former exploitation of the peasants. An army report described how one soldier became so frenzied while attending one of the sessions that he collapsed physically and mentally. When he came round, he was a gibbering wreck.

There is a remarkable illustration of Mao Zedong's personal involvement in the suppression of the peasantry. In 1947, Mao sent his oldest son, Anying, whom he had always regarded as too meek, to take part in the proceedings in order to sharpen his revolutionary edge. Anying was certainly a sensitive type; he was shattered by what he observed and suffered a mental breakdown. In his diary, he recorded how the people from a group of neighbouring villages who had shown insufficient enthusiasm for the CCP's methods were made to attend an anti-landlord rally. The villagers were held for five days in an open area, which they were not permitted to leave. It was midwinter, with the temperature below freezing point, and some died from exposure. Yet despite the cold the villagers finally warmed to their task. They began to chant Maoist slogans and scream abuse at the landlords who were made to kneel before them. On the fifth day, to the accompaniment of concerted yells of 'Kill, Kill, Kill!', the crowd, using fists, feet and wooden

When not beaten to death by the crowd, the convicted landlord would be shot. Between 1945 and 1950, some one million landlords died at the CCP's hands. (Philip Jowett)

sticks, beat the eight pinioned landlords to death. Mao Anying recorded in his diary that the experience left him 'so full of pain' that he wept continuously. He wrote that his anguish was intensified by his awareness that the soldiers and party officials responsible for organizing the terrifying scenes he had witnessed were drawn from what he called 'the dregs of society'.

Of course, not all Communists came from the dregs of society. Some had feelings of revulsion, similar to Anying's, about the land reforms they were implementing. Indeed, some CCP members appealed to Mao Zedong to intervene to lessen the brutality in the countryside. They were taking a risk; he might well have turned on them. But in this instance Mao acknowledged their grievance. He agreed that 'killing without discrimination is entirely wrong' since 'this would only cause our Party to forfeit sympathy and become alienated from the masses'. While admitting to no fault on his own part, he accepted that those lower down the chain of command had been guilty of blurring the distinction between 'what was permissible and what was not'. Mao instructed Liu Shaoqi, one of his most trusted senior commanders, to take the blame on behalf of the top Party officials. Liu duly did so. He admitted that the PLA's 'liberation' policies during the Civil War too often involved 'indiscriminate beating and killing'. He told the comrades in a circular intended for Party eyes only that he had allowed excesses to occur, but that Mao in his perceptive wisdom had spotted these and called a halt to them.

The Communists' ferocious land reform programme, which even Mao admitted had gone too far, ought to have given the Nationalists the opportunity to recover lost popularity with the peasants. But, with the blindness that was to characterize the GMD's dealings with the people throughout the Civil War, they were as brutal in their own way as the Communists. The Nationalists diverted 150,000 troops to recover the villages liberated under the CCP's reform programme. Their task was to oversee the restoration to the surviving landlord families of the properties taken from them by the Communists. Again, it was a bitter affair. Accompanied by NRA squads, former landlords called on their former tenants and demanded full payment of the rent owing to them since they had been dispossessed by the Communists. Peasants who refused were beaten and shot. Village leaders who had willingly joined in the CCP's land reforms were buried alive as a warning to the peasants of the perils of co-operation with the Communists.

The PLA sought to exploit the reaction that the Nationalists' methods had created among the people. It was greatly aided in this by Lin Biao, one of the PLA's ablest generals, who proved an indispensable contributor to the Communist victories in the decisive Liaoshen and Pinjin campaigns. Lin's forces contained special propaganda detachments, whose main task was to think of ways that could persuade the waverers in the NRA ranks to give up and come over to them. Pamphlets with simple messages to this effect were smuggled into or dropped over enemy lines:

> Brothers, lay down your arms which you never wanted to take up. Did you join the Guomindang army freely? No, you were dragged into it at the end of a rope. Come over to us. If you want, we will send you home. Better still, you can join us and fight to free your homes as we have ours.

As the propaganda indicated, an important aspect of the Communists' attitude was their developing conviction that they were morally superior to the Nationalists. Their survival after decades of precarious existence, in

A Communist sympathiser is mistreated by Nationalist forces. (Photo © Hulton-Deutsch Collection/CORBIS/Corbis via Getty Images)

Mao Anying, whose tragic life ended with his death while serving with the PLA in Korea in 1950. Anying's death was said to be the last time Mao was truly moved emotionally. (Historic Collection / Alamy Stock Photo)

which they had thwarted the attempts of the Japanese and the GMD to destroy them, gave them a powerful self-belief. This was reinforced by the teachings of Mao Zedong, who, during the Yanan years, had formulated the notion that the Chinese Communists were a providential force. They still had to win on the field of battle, of course, but insofar as high morale is a winning factor in war, the advantages were very much with the Communists.

The PLA commanders

An undoubted advantage that Mao had over Chiang was the loyalty of his commanders. While the GMD leader struggled throughout the war with insubordination among the military and was often

betrayed by senior personnel who passed information to the Communists, Mao was seldom faced with opposition. The outstanding characteristic of Mao's major colleagues, Lin Biao, Zhu De, Zhou Enlai and Liu Shaoqi, was their commitment to him as military leader. This extended to their allowing the credit for their own ideas and military successes to go to him. They were sometimes dubious about the correctness of Mao's judgements, but there was no case of their defying him once he had made a clear decision.

In the spring of 1945 at a major Party congress in Yanan, the CCP, in preparation for the renewed Civil War that they knew was coming, had set up a Central Military Committee, composed of some 80 members appointed from the upper ranks of the Party. This in turn appointed an inner group, known as the Secretariat, which, under the ultimate authority of Mao Zedong as Chairman, was responsible for running the war. The chief members of this Committee were Zhu De (Chu Teh), Zhou Enlai (Chou En-lai) and Liu Shaoqi (Liu Shao-chi).

Zhu De

An experienced commander whose military links with Mao went back to the time of the Long March, Zhu had had his differences over strategy with Mao in those early times. Mao had wanted to preserve the CCP's strength by avoiding pitched battles with the Japanese, while Zhu had been eager to increase the CCP's military reputation by taking on the enemy. One result of Zhu's approach had been a bad mauling of the Red Army by the Japanese in 1941. This left a mark against Zhu's name. While it did not permanently damage him, since he continued to be an inspiring and successful general, it was always something that Mao was prepared to bring up to keep Zhu in his place. What also limited Zhu's influence was his relative lack of interest in politics. His training and instincts were military and he had no real taste for the political infighting that promotion within the CCP required.

OPPOSITE
Communist fighters in 1945 carrying a mixture of old and new weapons, most of which were captured Japanese stock passed on by the Soviet forces. (AirSeaLand Photos)

Mao Zedong and Zhu De in discussion in Yanan in 1945. (Photo by: Universal History Archive/UIG via Getty Images)

Yet it was Zhu De who was primarily responsible for modernizing the PLA from 1945 onwards. Zhu's aim was to develop the various guerrilla units that formed the PLA into an integrated and cohesive force. He believed effective communications to be essential in this; hence his emphasis on the production of radios and signalling systems and the training of troops in their use. The Communists must also, he urged, have their own regular supply of equipment and weaponry. Until they had these they could not truly modernize – it was no longer sufficient to rely on capturing weapons from the enemy. The particular weaponry that Zhu demanded was artillery. His experience fighting both the Japanese and the Nationalists had convinced him that it was the PLA's lack of firepower that so often restricted them to merely harassing rather than defeating the enemy: 'our fighters often encounter pillboxes and temporary earthworks, common in mobile warfare, which keep them from gaining victory'. Zhu insisted that only with both light and heavy artillery and a reliable supply of shells would the PLA be able to develop effective assault tactics against fortified positions. Until that capability was achieved there was no realistic chance of seizing the urban areas of China, a prerequisite for winning the Civil War.

One of Zhu's most interesting contributions to the Red Army was his insistence on practical responses and tactics. He had little time for the sloganizing that turned campaigns into a matter of trying to apply Mao's political sayings to the battlefield: 'Rid the ranks of all impotent thinking' or 'The Party commands the gun, the gun must never be allowed to command the Party'. Zhu saw little military value in seeking to inspire his troops in the heat of battle with such vague promptings. But this did not mean that he openly defied Mao on the political front. That was not his intention; his concerns were military. Mao for his part shrewdly judged that Zhu's talents as a soldier were what mattered. As long as Zhu proved successful, Mao was prepared to trust him. There was a sense in which military success became its own justification. To have held a position or made gains was a powerful argument for the correctness of the tactics that had produced that result. So it was as a tactician rather than as a strategist that Zhu was of greatest value to the Red Army. Although Mao consulted him on strategy, Zhu played a relatively small role in the planning of the grand designs.

Zhou Enlai

A second key member of the Secretariat, Zhou Enlai was seldom involved in directing operations; his great value to Mao lay in his diplomatic skills. Urbane and multilingual, Zhou up to 1945 had acted as the CCP's chief negotiator with the GMD, the Russians and the Americans. From 1945, Zhou, a master of discretion, employed his persuasive arts to prevent disagreements

Zhou Enlai stands behind Mao, as he always loyally did. Zhou played a vital role in maintaining harmony among the PLA commanders. (AFP via Getty Images)

among CCP commanders from developing into serious military differences. His most marked characteristic was his loyalty to Mao. There is no example of Zhou ever opposing his leader on a key issue. This was a huge asset to Mao. It meant that his two principal lieutenants, Zhou Enlai and Zhu De, were committed to him in a manner that created an imposing example for all lesser commanders and made serious opposition difficult if not unthinkable.

Lin Biao

Lin was to die in an air crash in 1971 while fleeing from China, after being implicated in a plot masterminded by his son, Lin Liguo, to assassinate Mao. Lin Biao's aim was to seek sanctuary in the USSR, but his British-made Trident plane crashed when it ran out of fuel before reaching the Soviet border. The execration in which Lin Biao's name was held thereafter wiped from public record all his previous achievements in promoting Mao and Chinese Communism. Yet these had been considerable. A colleague of Mao since the 1920s, and the principal of the Anti-Japanese University at Yanan, Lin had won glory for himself and the CCP in 1937 by inflicting on the Japanese one of the few major defeats they suffered in China. Lin was later wounded and out of action for

Mao (right) recognised Lin Biao (left) as one of the PLA's ablest and most effective Civil War generals. After 1949, Lin was the chief creator of the cult of Mao Zedong. (Photo by: Universal History Archive/UIG via Getty Images)

the last years of the struggle against Japan. However, having recovered, he returned to prominent command during the Civil War. While never openly defying Mao's strategic decisions, he did show considerable independence of judgement. That Mao was willing to accept this suggests he regarded Lin as among the most gifted of his commanders.

Liu Shaoqi

It was Liu Shaoqi's tragedy that he came to be hated by Mao in the 1960s. In destroying Liu politically during the Cultural Revolution of that era, Mao effectively erased the contribution Liu had made to the winning of the Civil War. Yet it had been Liu who devised what proved to be the highly successful CCP strategy in Manchuria, which proved to be the turning point in the war. Moreover, he had been responsible for turning the liberated areas into sustainable administrative regions rather than mere military bases. It was largely on Liu's initiative that the PLA developed what became known as the 'march on the north, defend in the south' strategy. Judging that the Communists could not fight successfully in all the regions where they were present, Liu put into operation plans for concentrating the PLA's main forces in the east central triangle of Shandong, Anhui and Henan, a move that proved instrumental in the CCP's eventual victory.

OPPOSITE
Liu Shaoqi. His later dismissal and disgrace during the Cultural Revolution in the 1960s obscured the fact that he had been one of the most resourceful of the PLA's Civil War strategists. (Photo by: Sovfoto/ Universal Images Group via Getty Images)

One of the difficulties for historians is knowing which strategies Mao initiated and which ones he simply appropriated. The documentary evidence is scanty, but it appears that whenever a particular approach proved successful Mao would assert that it had been his thinking all along. Such was his political control that there was little point, and much danger, in his commanders' laying claim to the original plan. A logical conclusion is that it was not so much Mao's military skills, though these are not to be underestimated, but the political control that he exercised, which established his reputation as a commander. In the 'rectification movement' of 1942–44, he had ruthlessly purged the

CCP and the Red Army by making even his highest-ranking colleagues and generals engage in humiliating public 'self-criticism', a form of ritual humiliation in which the individual knelt in front of his colleagues and confessed to having failed to be totally committed to the performance of his revolutionary duties. After such confession, it was no longer legitimate or possible for the individual to challenge Mao openly. This hard reality deterred his military commanders from vying with Mao for acclaim even when their successes merited it.

THE FIGHTING

Strategy and tactics

Prelude

In the period between the Japanese surrender in August 1945 and the renewal of the Chinese Civil War in June 1946, an unreal peace prevailed. Officially the Communists and the Nationalists observed a truce, but in reality they were preparing for war against each other. The truce had been a product of talks between Mao Zedong and Chiang Kai-shek that had begun in August 1945. Conducted under American auspices and initially backed by Stalin and the Soviet Union, the talks were held in Chongqing (Chungking), the Nationalist stronghold on the Yangzi (Yangtze) River. Mao had flown there from his Yanan base; fearing that the plane might be sabotaged on this, his first-ever flight, he had insisted that Patrick Hurley, the chief American representative, accompany him. Despite the talks lasting six weeks, Mao never lost the misgivings with which he had set out.

It was no surprise, therefore, when the talks stalled with a nominal truce still operating but no agreement reached on any major issue. Hurley returned home a disappointed man, asserting that it was primarily Chiang's obduracy that made a settlement impossible. President Truman, however, still believed that a compromise could be achieved. He sent the USA's most distinguished soldier and diplomat, General George Marshall, to try to broker a lasting agreement. In December 1945, Marshall persuaded the two Chinese sides to meet again to negotiate. This second round of talks, held this time in Nanjing, the GMD's restored capital, was given the grand name of a Consultative Conference, but it was not a success. Among the many stumbling blocks was the GMD's concern that the Communists, while willing formally to recognize Chiang Kai-shek as the legitimate leader of China, were not willing to abide by this in practice. On the Communists' side there was deep doubt that the Nationalist regime would honour its promise to allow them to retain the liberated areas that they now held. It was their fear over this that led the Communists to walk out of the talks.

The plain truth was that neither side trusted the other. Even as they talked, they were seizing territory and making ready for renewed fighting. It was the mutual distrust between the CCP and the GMD that finally exasperated the Americans and led to their abandoning

Mao (second left), the US Ambassador to China Patrick Hurley (centre), and Zhou Enlai (far right) at Yanan in 1945, shortly before flying to meet Chiang Kai-shek for talks. (Philip Jowett)

the attempt to act as mediators. Yet the US mission did not finally withdraw until January 1947. Its efforts to achieve a resolution during its last year in China had a highly significant, though unintended, consequence. In June 1946, Marshall had managed to get the two sides to agree to a ceasefire in Manchuria, a region that, since it was not technically part of China proper, had not been included in the truce that had fitfully operated since the Chongqing talks in 1945. Although this new ceasefire lasted only six weeks, it fundamentally altered the balance between the GMD and CCP.

To appreciate why this was so important it has to be understood that Chiang had made his first military objective the recovery of Manchuria. He had calculated that if the GMD could recover this huge region, it would effectively destroy the CCP's influence in northern China, the only area where the Communists had strong bases. That was why, at the conclusion of the Japanese war, Chiang had immediately begun sending troops into Manchuria. This process was quickened following the Soviet Union's withdrawal of its army from Manchuria in May 1946. Chiang targeted and took Changchun,

Mao and Chiang toasting each other before the breakdown of their talks in 1946. Their smiles belied their antipathy. (Bettmann/Getty Images)

the capital city of Jilin province. Mao Zedong responded immediately. Knowing that it was vital to control at least one major urban area in Manchuria, he directed Lin Biao to occupy Harbin, Heilongjiang's capital city. By early May it was in Communist hands.

Nevertheless, the GMD's attempt to impose itself on the region had put the Communists under great pressure and they had been forced to give ground. There was no guarantee that they could continue to hold Harbin. That is what made Chiang's agreement to a ceasefire in Manchuria in the summer of 1946 so critical. The lull in the fighting gave Mao's forces an opportunity to strengthen their position and wipe out the gains the Nationalists had recently made there. From being on the point of withdrawing from Harbin, their toehold in Manchuria, the Communists were able to turn about and over the next two weeks of the truce take over a large area that extended to the border with the USSR.

The main phases of the Civil War

The Civil War had three essential phases. The first was the NRA's attempt to take the initiative by seizing the main Communist bases in Manchuria and north-eastern China in 1946–47. In the second phase, the PLA successfully repulsed these attacks. In the third phase, the Communists took the offensive from 1947 onwards by moving south to occupy the previously Nationalist-held areas of central and southern China.

Within these phases were five major campaigns which ultimately determined the outcome of the Civil War:

* The struggle for Manchuria, 1946–47
* The 'strongpoint offensive', 1947
* The Liaoshen campaign, September–November 1948
* The Huaihai campaign, November 1948–January 1949
* The Pingjin campaign, November 1948–January 1949

The struggle for Manchuria

Even before the brief ceasefire had given the initiative to the PLA, the Nationalists had experienced great problems in trying to impose themselves on the region. Manchuria, equal in size to Western Europe and made up of three main provinces, Heilongjiang, Jilin and Liaoning, had for 14 years after 1931 been the Japanese puppet state of Manchuguo. When Japan surrendered in 1945, the Nationalists had thus inherited what had been an efficient, albeit coercive, administration. But they were unable to sustain it. The GMD troops, flown in by the Americans, were not welcomed as liberators. The administrators whom Chiang appointed had little understanding of local conditions and peoples. Widespread resistance from the peasants to the GMD's attempt to impose itself was exploited by the Communists, who presented themselves as defenders of the people.

A key factor in the PLA's harassing of the Nationalists was the amount of help they received from local civilians, who destroyed telegraph and telephone lines and tore up sections of railway in order to disrupt GMD troop movements. By 1947 over 10,000 miles of railway line had been sabotaged. Deprived of reliable communications and faced with sniping and guerrilla attacks in the countryside, for which they lacked adequate detailed maps, the GMD commanders preferred to keep their troops safe within the fortified walled compounds in the towns. In effect, they became besieged in their own bases in Manchuria. It was an inglorious policy and effectively handed Manchuria back to the Communists. The region would continue to be disputed between the CCP and the GMD, but Chiang's failure to recover Manchuria in the first stage of the war revealed how limited support was for his regime.

Chiang's decision to send the GMD's major forces into Manchuria before he had secured the supply lines necessary to keep his armies fully equipped was the basic misjudgement from which all his later military problems stemmed. His decision ran counter to the advice of

MANCHURIA

N

0   250 miles
0   500 km

USSR

USSR

Inner
Mongolia

Heilongjiang

MONGOLIA

Harbin

Inner
Mongolia

Changchun

Jilin

Vladivostok

Jilin

Siping

Jinzhou

Shenyang

Liaoning

SEA
OF
JAPAN

Beijing

Tianjin

Lushun

YELLOW
SEA

many of his military leaders who were rightly concerned that unless the supply lines were established, the NRA would be highly vulnerable in a region of China where the Communists were at their strongest.

Harbin

Once successfully established in Harbin, the CCP turned it into its chief base in Manchuria. It was the first major urban success story in the CCP's history and became the organizational model for the other cities and towns that the Communists came to occupy. A city of some 800,000 people, Harbin was divided into six districts, which were in turn sub-divided into smaller zones. Each was tightly organized, with Party control reaching right down to street level where surveillance units monitored local activity and acted as a police force. Constant propaganda through newspapers, radio broadcasts, banners and posters extolled the virtues of the city's new regime. The commercial businesses that were permitted to continue were heavily taxed and required to shape their activities according to CCP demands. The local people had to contribute money and labour for the upkeep of the Communist armies. Movement into and out of the city and movement within it was strictly controlled by the issuing of travel permits. Proof of the effectiveness of such controls was Harbin's ability to survive an outbreak of bubonic plague in 1947. Although some 30,000 inhabitants died, the public health measures imposed by the Communist authorities restricted the spread of the disease and prevented it from devastating the city.

Harbin was also of vital military significance. After securing the city, Mao, in consultation with his military commanders, principally Lin Biao, Chen Yi and He Long, developed a basic strategy that sought to increase the CCP's hold in Manchuria and northern China while withdrawing from most of central China above the Yangzi River. Mao's stated belief was 'If we have Manchuria, our victory will be guaranteed'. His words were to prove prophetic, as Manchuria was to be the key

to the Communists' ultimate success in 1949. It was the area where they were at their strongest and so able to match the Nationalists in manpower and resources.

Manchuria also had the advantage of being the most industrially advanced region of China, a legacy of its long occupation by the Japanese. Although the Soviet forces had, during their 1945–46 occupation, stripped it of as much of its industrial plant as could be moved, the region still remained a major prize in Mao's eyes. Manchuria's long border with the USSR also appeared to offer a safe haven to which the Communists could withdraw. Employing a simile to describe the CCP's comfortable position in Manchuria in 1946, Mao likened Mongolia and North Korea to the supportive sides of an armchair with the Soviet border providing the back rest.

Well-equipped PLA troops prepare to ambush the enemy outside Harbin. (AirSeaLand Photos)

It was the CCP's grip on Harbin that enabled Lin Biao to develop the Communist army in Manchuria. Lin's was a new army with new ideas. It was no longer simply the set of guerrilla detachments that had made up Mao's forces in the previous struggles against the Nationalists and the Japanese. Lin's objective was to build an army of trained and equipped divisions, capable of sustained warfare against large-scale enemy forces. Harbin provided him with the space in which to prepare such an army. The fruits of Lin's endeavours were evident in his repulsing of the Nationalist forces when they tried to take Harbin in the early months of 1947.

Under heavy pressure from NRA counter-attacks in the winter of 1946/47, the Communists had to give up over 150 towns, including Zhangjiakou, and had fallen back before the GMD advance northward from the Shanhaiguan pass. The Nationalists, judging that the bitter seasonal weather of the region would delay any chance of Communist recovery, had set up winter quarters south of the frozen Sungari River, not expecting any serious fighting until the spring. Using surprise to his advantage, Lin sent his forces across the ice to attack the Nationalists in their own base. Forced to fall back, the Nationalists were further staggered by the scale of the assault that Lin then launched. A force of nearly 400,000 Communists attempted to seize the key railway junction of Siping. Chiang Kai-shek rushed land and aerial forces north to prevent its loss. The Reds retreated but not before they had taken possession of hundreds of thousands of abandoned Nationalist weapons. The daring of Lin's attack had shown that Chiang's notion of the Communists as mere rural bandits who could be steadily mopped up was now hopelessly unrealistic.

Despite their reverses in Manchuria, the Nationalists had not suffered a major defeat. They still had the overall advantage in numbers and were still in possession of Shenyang, the capital of Liaoning province. They also held a number of key lines of communication, which gave them control of northern China. Three of these fanned out from Beijing:

KEY PASSES AND CORRIDORS, 1947–49

MONGOLIA

Inner Mongolia

Sungari River

N

Shenyang

Zhangjiakou

2

Jinzhou

1

Liaoning

NORTH KOREA

Beijing

3

Hebei

Taiyuan

KOREA BAY

Shanxi

Yellow River

4

Jinan

SOUTH KOREA

Shandong

Qingdao

YELLOW SEA

Nanjing

Shanghai

1 Beijing to Shenyang corridor with the Shanhaiguan Pass

2 Beijing to Zhangjiakou

3 Beijing to Taiyuan

4 Jinan to Qingdao

Nationalist-held areas

Communist-held areas

| 0 | 250 miles |
| 0 | 500 km |

- the route between Beijing via the Shanhaiguan pass to Shenyang;
- the south-western corridor linking Beijing and Taiyuan, where the army of the pro-GMD Shanxi warlord, Yan Xishan, was stationed; and
- the railway line that ran north-west from Beijing to Zhangjiakou.

Another major route under Nationalist control was that between Jinan on the Yellow River and Qingdao. It was to be the loss of these passes to the PLA that eventually ended the GMD's grip on northern China.

Despite the appearance of control that the presence of 200,000 Nationalist troops in northern China gave Chiang, the reality was that with the successful PLA defence of Harbin the initiative had passed to the Communists. The Nationalists' superior air power was nullified by the destruction of the airstrips and runways that the PLA found so easy to attack and the NRA so hard to defend. Similarly, the repeated sabotage of the railway lines made the large-scale movement of Nationalist troops extremely difficult. But it was the loss of the airfields that proved decisive. Chiang was unable to provide the air cover to protect his forces on the ground or launch aerial attacks on Communist positions. Early in 1947, the freelance American air ace Claire Chennault tried to come to the Nationalists' assistance by flying in supplies. During the Pacific War, Chennault had led his squadron of 'Flying Tigers' in a series of daring sorties against the Japanese. However, his impressive efforts to do the same against the Communists, although equally courageous, brought only partial relief to the beleaguered GMD positions.

Yanan and the 'strongpoint offensive'

In March 1947 GMD forces captured Yanan, the Communist base to which Mao had fled at the end of the Long March, and where, over the next decade, he had constructed a Chinese Communist soviet. A few months later, to luxuriate in the capture, Chiang Kai-shek flew into Yanan and walked along the streets and into the cave dwellings where Mao had once lived. The Nationalists hailed this as a great triumph, which would be the prelude to their recovery from the loss of Manchuria. For a short period the taking of Yanan raised Nationalist morale, and territorial gains were made in Shanxi and neighbouring provinces. Some observers

OPPOSITE
PLA troops giving the Communist salute. The PLA helped to build morale and a sense of mission in its troops by encouraging them to engage enthusiastically in such military rituals. (Bettmann/Getty Images)

Mao rides out from Yanan in March 1947, leaving Chiang Kai-shek an empty city and a hollow victory. Mao's readiness to abandon the soviet base was a striking example of his pragmatic approach to war. (AFP via Getty Images)

noted around this time that Mao's manoeuvres often made himself very visible in order to draw fire from the NRA batteries, thereby exposing their positions. Others claimed that this was a Communist myth.

Yet what Chiang had intended as a great symbolic act of liberation proved an empty success. Mao had received forewarning of the impending attack on Yanan. Remarkably, the leaked intelligence appeared to have come from the office of the NRA general who led the attack, Hu Zongnan (Hu Tsung-nan). Although an admirer of Chiang Kai-shek personally, Hu had Communist sympathies which compromised his military conduct. The presence of such moles and informers in the Nationalist armies was a problem that would undermine Chiang throughout the Civil War.

LEFT
Hu Zongnan,
who played an
ambiguous role in
the Civil War; he
was both an NRA
commander and a
crypto-Communist.
(Photo by Paul
Popper/Popperfoto
via Getty Images)

BELOW
Hu Zongnan's
troops in training.
Despite betraying
the Nationalists over
Yanan, Hu continued
to profess loyalty to
Chiang and to lead
a Nationalist army.
(Philip Jowett)

No matter who had passed on the information, the fact was that by the time the Nationalist forces reached Yanan it was a deserted city. Acting on Mao's instructions, Peng Dehuai, commander of the PLA's northwest field army, had fought a holding action just south of the city against the advanced units of the approaching NRA force. This had given time for the bulk of the Communist forces to withdraw, taking their essential equipment with them. Although at the time forced upon Mao by circumstance, the abandonment of Yanan became part of Mao's policy to leave the Nationalists only meaningless victories. He told his commanders: 'We should not try to stop them. Chiang thinks when he has seized the devils' lair, he will win. In fact, he will lose everything. We will give Chiang Yanan. He will give us China.'

Peng Dehuai. Impressed by Peng as a military theorist who emphasised the value of counter-offensives, Mao made him commander of the northwest field army. (Photo by United States Information Agency/ PhotoQuest/Getty Images)

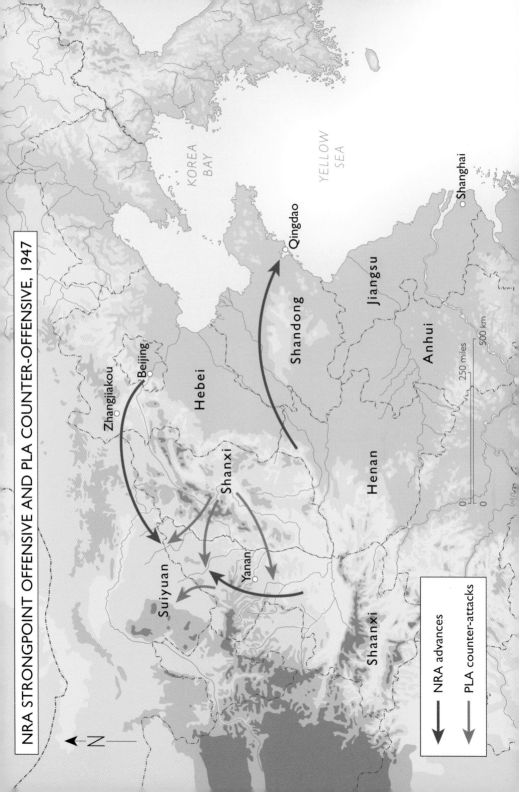

NRA STRONGPOINT OFFENSIVE AND PLA COUNTER-OFFENSIVE, 1947

KOREA BAY

YELLOW SEA

Shanghai

Qingdao

Shandong

Jiangsu

Beijing

Zhangjiakou

Hebei

Anhui

Shanxi

Henan

Suiyuan

Yanan

Shaanxi

500 km

250 miles

N

NRA advances

PLA counter-attacks

The GMD's taking of Yanan belonged to a larger strategic picture. Chiang, judging that he had gained control of the main regions of Hebei, switched his attack to Shandong and Shanxi. This 'strongpoint offensive', as the GMD referred to it, proved to be a major error. Adopting it involved the Nationalists overstretching their lines with the result that, although they often held superior positions, they were unable to concentrate their forces in such a way as to inflict a major defeat on the enemy. As the intended offensive petered out, Lin Biao and Nie Rongzhen led the Communists in a series of counter-attacks. So successful were these that they marked a key stage in the Civil War. The GMD had effectively lost north-eastern China; the initiative had passed to the Communists. It was an initiative they were never to surrender.

The success of the counter-offensive convinced Mao that it was time to alter the strategy with which he had begun the war. By the time the Nationalists took Yanan, the Communists had already begun to build a new base around Zhangjiakou in Hebei province. It was from there that Mao directed the next stage of the strategy, which was aimed at exhausting the Nationalist armies. In 1946 he had judged that, since his forces were outnumbered and less well equipped than the GMD's, his tactics would have to be essentially a continuation of the hit-and-run guerrilla methods he had customarily followed. He had seen the Civil War developing as a long attritional struggle. However, the failure of Chiang's 'strongpoint offensive' convinced Mao that the Communists could now carry the battle to the enemy and win outright against the Nationalists. There were divisions of opinion within the CCP over this, between those who, following Mao's lead, wanted to follow an offensive strategy and those, like Lin Biao and Chen Yi, a Long March veteran, who wanted time to build up their forces and who therefore argued for the continuation of what they called 'mobile defence'.

Interestingly, although Mao was the presiding genius, he did allow considerable operational freedom to his commanders in the field. He was invariably willing to

OPPOSITE
PLA commander Nie Rongzhen, who played a key role in the Communist takeover of north-eastern China. (CPA Media Pte Ltd / Alamy Stock Photo)

let them adjust their tactics in the light of the actual position in which they found themselves. He provided the broad strategic lines but gave them latitude to follow their instincts and operational judgements. This did not mean that he was ever anything other than the ultimate military authority. He retained the reins of power.

The decisive campaigns, 1948–49

The Liaoshen (Liaoning–Shenyang) campaign, September–November 1948

In the summer of 1948, the Civil War entered its most decisive and destructive stage. Mao, who had established his military HQ at Xibaipo in Hebei province, where he stayed between May 1948 and March 1949, was convinced that the tide had turned and was flowing strongly in his favour. He ordered his commanders to abandon 'mobile defence' and undertake the GMD's 'total destruction'. Gone now was any notion of a compromise peace. In response, Lin Biao, having taken time to build up his forces, targeted the last two major cities in Manchuria to which the Nationalists still clung – Changchun and Shenyang. But before either of those cities could be taken the Nationalist base of Jinzhou needed to be destroyed, since as a key railway junction it linked Beijing to the two northern cities.

Aware of the threat, Chiang flew to Shenyang to take direct command. Nearly a quarter of a million NRA troops were diverted to defend Jinzhou. All to no avail; despite suffering heavy casualties in their attack, the surrounding PLA forces, which under Lin Biao had become increasingly proficient in artillery use, ceaselessly fired shells into Jinzhou until the defences were broken. Fierce close-quarter combat followed as the PLA advanced street by street until, on 15 October, the GMD, already severely weakened by large numbers of desertions, finally surrendered.

A similar fate soon befell Changchun. Under siege since August, the Nationalists had tried to break out on several

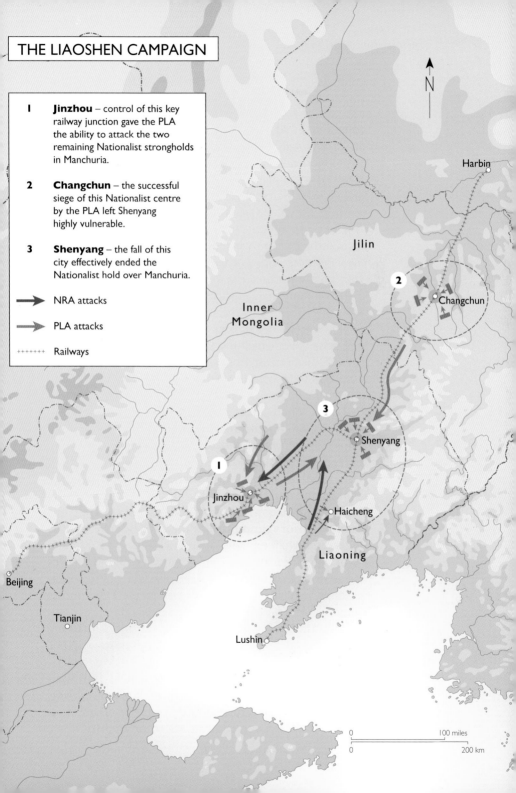

THE LIAOSHEN CAMPAIGN

1   **Jinzhou** – control of this key railway junction gave the PLA the ability to attack the two remaining Nationalist strongholds in Manchuria.

2   **Changchun** – the successful siege of this Nationalist centre by the PLA left Shenyang highly vulnerable.

3   **Shenyang** – the fall of this city effectively ended the Nationalist hold over Manchuria.

→   NRA attacks

→   PLA attacks

+++++++   Railways

N

Harbin

Jilin

2 Changchun

Inner Mongolia

3

Shenyang

1

Jinzhou

Haicheng

Liaoning

Beijing

Tianjin

Lushin

0   100 miles

0   200 km

occasions but had been unable to pierce the surrounding PLA ring. After three months of fearful privation that reduced the population to cannibalism, with corpses being bought and sold for food, Changchun finally surrendered on 26 October. The Nationalist cause had not been well served by their leaders at Changchun. A number of NRA officers made contact with the enemy, offering to come over to their side. Mao sent personal orders that any Nationalist deserters should be accepted into the PLA and allowed to retain their officer rank. Some of the defecting officers advised the PLA on where the weakest points were in the city's defences and where the survivors were sheltering. They then supervised the shelling of these areas. The city's death toll numbered a quarter of a million. It was said that so many bodies lay in the surrounding marshland, where would-be escapers had been shot down, that they created a causeway over which the PLA crossed into the city. The 100,000 Nationalist troops who had fought to the end, including their commander, Zheng Dongguao, became PLA prisoners.

Zhang Zhenglong, a PLA colonel, later confessed that the Communist troops had deliberately massacred thousands of civilians after the siege was over. He recalled: 'Changchun was like Hiroshima. The casualties were about the same. Hiroshima took nine seconds; Changchun took five months.' The book in which he made the admission was published in China in 1989 but was immediately suppressed by the Chinese government. However, in 2006, substance was added to Zhang's claim when excavators came across 160,000 bodies dating from the time of the siege of Changchun, which appeared to have been hastily buried by the Communist victors.

With their loss of Changchun, the Nationalists now faced an even more daunting question as to whether they could keep hold of their last base in Manchuria, Shenyang, which stood isolated now that its link with Beijing had been cut with the fall of Jinzhou. Chiang Kai-shek, who had returned to Beijing, was determined to deny the PLA the final great Manchurian prize.

There was confusion in the GMD high command. Some, including Chiang, believed that a committed and successful defence of Shenyang was the only way to offset the gains made by the Communists. Others argued that to risk another struggle and defeat on the scale of Jinzhou and Changchun would play into the hands of the PLA, which now outnumbered the NRA and held better strategic positions. The decision on whether to stand and fight at Shenyang or move out and face the PLA on more advantageous ground was taken out of the Nationalists' hands by the speed with which the Communist forces moved to encircle the city. Lin Biao, having taken Jinzhou, led his forces north to cut off Shenyang. A Nationalist force, the New 1st Army, was sent under Liao Yaoxiang to relieve Shenyang but found itself outflanked by Lin's army as it approached the city. In a nine-day battle from 20 October to the 28th at Heishan, the 1st Army was decimated, Liao was captured and the Nationalists lost 100,000 men overall.

Wei Lihuang, Chiang's commander-in-chief in the north-east, whose disputes with his fellow officers weakened his leadership and who in effect surrendered Shenyang. (Photo by Photo12/UIG/Getty Images)

Shenyang now lay largely unprotected. By the end of October the Nationalists were surrounded on all the approaches to the city. With scant relief provided by air drops and supplies flown in, it became apparent that Shenyang had little chance of holding out. The Nationalists' predicament was compounded by confusion and betrayal among their commanders. Wei Lihuang, Chiang's commander-in-chief in the north-east, abruptly left Shenyang by plane, passing on the direct responsibility for Shenyang's defence to Zhou Fucheng.

It was a poisoned chalice. The approach of the PLA and the lack of leadership among the Nationalist military produced an uncontrollable panic within the city. The violent fighting in the streets over dwindling food stocks and for the places on the last trains and aircraft to leave Shenyang illustrated the impossibility of organizing any form of effective defence. By the time the PLA broke into the city on 1 November there was only token resistance; the Nationalist resolve had evaporated. The formal surrender followed on 2 November.

The fall of Shenyang marked the culmination of the Liaoshen campaign, a campaign that within a period of three months had seen the defeat of the GMD in the three major battles of Changchun, Jinzhou and Shenyang, and in scores of smaller but connected engagements. The NRA had lost over 400,000 men through casualties and desertions. Scarcely 150,000 troops were able to escape south to regroup. But it was more than a series of military defeats. In strategic terms it meant that the Communists now controlled Manchuria, the first great prize in the Civil War.

Chiang himself referred to its loss as a 'world catastrophe'. It was a certainly a Nationalist catastrophe. In 1946, Chiang had calculated that if his Nationalists took Manchuria, it would re-establish their dominance and be the first step towards realizing his aim of controlling the whole of China. But now, two years later, the position had been precisely reversed. Having taken Manchuria, the Communists had effective control of north-east China.

This was now the base from which they could plan the campaigns to dislodge the Nationalists from the rest of the mainland. The mentality of the two sides had changed. From the Liaoshen campaign onwards, the PLA were on the attack and the NRA were in retreat. Chiang's thoughts turned to saving something by returning to the idea of a compromise settlement. He made overtures to both the Americans and the USSR as to whether they would consider acting as brokers again between the GMD and the Communists. But the time for that had passed. The war was swinging too strongly in the PLA's favour for Mao to consider such a proposal. He wanted the destruction of the GMD and believed that this was now achievable.

The Huaihai campaign, November 1948–January 1949

There was a well-known saying among Chinese strategists: 'Manchuria is a limb of the nation, the central provinces are the heart.' In that saying lay the explanation for what proved to be the pivotal struggle of the Civil War, the Huaihai campaign, so called because the bulk of the fighting occurred in the region between the Huai River and the Longhai railway. The prelude to the campaign was Chiang Kai-shek's decision, in response to the loss of Manchuria, to withdraw the bulk of his troops from Shandong province with the aim of preventing further southward movement by the Communists into the central provinces. Chiang judged that what was at stake was nothing less than the possession of 'China's heart'.

Chiang chose to group his forces around the city of Xuzhou, a key junction on the Longhai railway that ran between the Yellow and the Yangzi rivers and connected the GMD capital, Nanjing, to the great port of Shanghai. He believed that Xuzhou was eminently defensible; the hills to the north of the city would slow the progress of any attackers, while the flatter land to the south would enable NRA supply lines to be maintained. Chiang also reckoned that he had time on his side, calculating that it would take months for the PLA to gather enough troops for a concerted attack.

NEXT PAGES
Chiang was formally installed as President of the Republic of China in May 1948. But by then, despite the trappings of power, he was beginning to lose the Civil War. (Bettmann/Getty Images)

Chiang was wrong. Mao had already made the critical decision not to wait for troop reinforcements from the north; he ordered Deng Xiaoping (Teng Hsiao-ping) immediately to enlist into the PLA the Nationalist troops who had either defected or been taken prisoner in the fighting in Shandong. Overruling the objections of those of his commanders who argued that this was too great a risk, Mao insisted that such augmentation of the PLA must now be a consistent policy. 'No prisoner will be let go. Most of them will be filled into our troops. The human resources for our troops to defeat Chiang mainly come from prisoners.' He told Deng Xiaoping and Liu Bocheng, his main campaign commanders, that unless this policy was followed the PLA would be unable to sustain its war effort.

Mao's urgency was explained by his understanding, which paralleled Chiang's, that the war had reached a critical stage. He grasped the momentous consequences that would ensue if the Nationalists, following their loss of Manchuria, could be dealt a further decisive blow in central China. It would leave them without a realistic hope of recovery. In arguably the most perceptive military judgement he was ever to take, Mao saw in the Huaihai campaign the chance to bring the war to a rapid and successful conclusion. It would justify his earlier decision to abandon attrition and embark on a war of total annihilation of the Nationalists.

True to his practice of rapidly promoting officers who had proved successful in the field, Mao entrusted the main planning of the Huaihai campaign to Su Yu, who had distinguished himself in the recent fighting in Shandong. Su believed that speed was vital. He wanted to engage the main Nationalist forces before they had time to move south and regroup – which, he judged, they would do if they realized that the enlarged PLA was intent on a pitched battle.

As happened in a number of key moments in the Civil War, the Nationalists were the cause of their own misfortunes. Disputes between commanders hindered effective liaison; even when workable plans

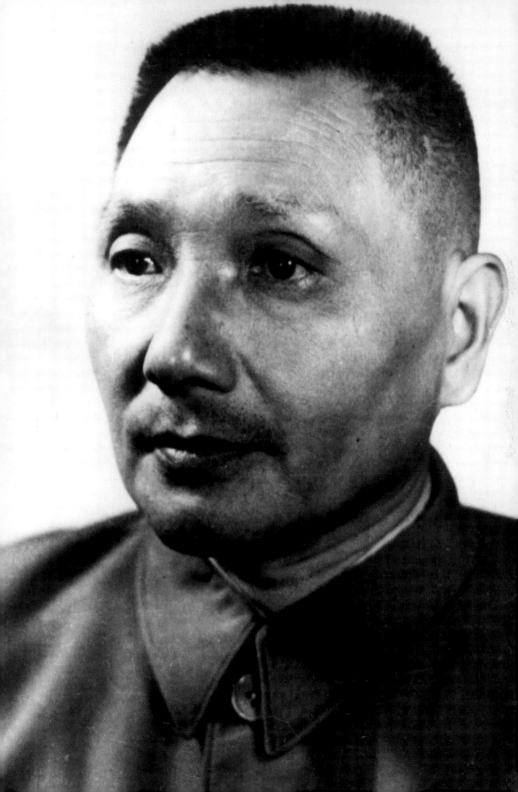

were drafted, these were in danger of being passed on to the Communists by moles within the GMD. Such was the case now. Su Yu received intelligence that told him of a major NRA troop movement that involved the 7th Army Group temporarily leaving Xuzhou to link up with an NRA force coming from the coast. Su ordered an immediate attack before the link could be made.

Within five days Xuzhou had been surrounded. The 7th Army Group under General Huang Baitao turned and tried to fight its way back into Xuzhou. It performed gamely but, cut off from supplies and reinforcements, it was pounded by heavy artillery for ten days before eventually being overwhelmed in late November at Zhanzhuan. Huang Baitao committed suicide. His army's defeat and his own tragic end might have been avoided had he received help from the newly formed 2nd NRA Army at Bengbu. However, although it had been in a position to assist, the 2nd Army had made no move. This was because its commander, Qiu Qinquan, nursed a grievance against Huang and so refused to commit his forces to a genuine relief effort. It was yet another of those feuds that so often undermined NRA effectiveness.

Not realizing the extent of the PLA's control, Chiang sent reinforcements north, only for these to be attacked and scattered south of Xuzhou by Deng Xiaoping's main force, which then went on to take Suxian. This left Xuzhou isolated. Meanwhile the PLA's East China Field Army, led by Chen Yi, had pushed its way up from the south, and the Central Plains Army under Liu Bocheng, known as 'the One-eyed Dragon' since he had been half-blinded in a grenade explosion, approached from the west. The combined Communist forces totalled some half a million troops. Yet the 300,000 Nationalist troops had an advantage in tanks, armoured vehicles and artillery. In the early stages of the fighting they held their own and inflicted severe casualties on some of the PLA units. However, heavy November rain turned much of the ground into quagmires, which made co-ordinated tank and vehicle movement impossible.

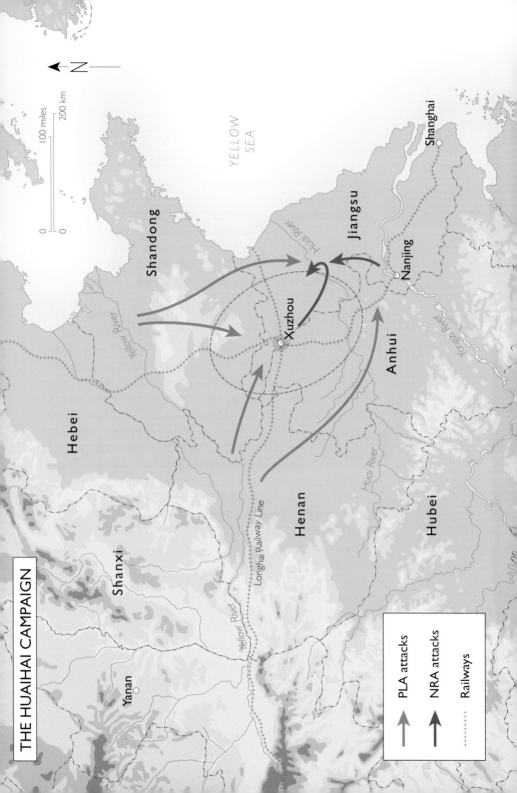

THE HUAIHAI CAMPAIGN

←N—

200 km

100 miles

YELLOW
SEA

Shandong

Jiangsu

Huai River

Nanjing

Shanghai

Xuzhou

Anhui

Yellow River

Hebei

Longhai Railway Line

Henan

Huai River

Hubei

Yangzi River

Shanxi

Yellow River

Yanan

PLA attacks

NRA attacks

+++++ Railways

Then in December the mud turned to snow-covered ruts as a bitter freeze set in.

Adding to the Nationalists' difficulties was their lack of effective air cover. Not only had they lost a large number of fighter aircraft in the recent Liaoshen campaign, which they had not had time to replace, but what planes they did have were prevented from flying by persistent snow falls, which obscured visibility. Deprived of supplies, the defenders began to run short of ammunition and food. The PLA's loudspeaker broadcasts promising the defenders food if they came over encouraged a growing number of desertions; starving soldiers and civilians slipped through the lines at night either to escape or to join the PLA.

The desertions showed the virtue of Mao's specific order, issued during the struggle for Xuzhou, that POWs be treated as potential recruits by offering them the chance of survival if they changed sides. In contrast, the Nationalists exercised no such calculated mercy. The severity of the fighting over Xuzhou made the taking of prisoners by the GMD impractical even had it been desirable. Henry Lieberman, an American newspaper reporter who travelled as an observer with one of Chiang's armies during the campaign, witnessed the grim practice followed by the Nationalists. He recorded that they frequently shot wounded PLA prisoners or left them to die, their justification being that they lacked sufficient medical facilities to treat their own troops, let alone the enemy's.

Liu Zhih, who had taken over command of the Nationalist campaign, ordered a counter-attack to try to pierce the PLA ring that had formed. His aim was not simply to save the beleaguered Nationalist forces but to protect Nanjing, the GMD capital, which the recent PLA successes had put under threat. Liu Zhih claimed that he was closing a deadly trap around the Communist forces, but it proved a vain boast. The deadly trap had been made by the PLA, not the Nationalists. To make its grip on Xuzhou unbreakable, the PLA had devastated a whole area, formed by a semi-circle whose radius stretched for 20 miles to the north of the city. Within that region villages had been razed and their people taken prisoner. A dark pall hung over the battle area as the columns of grey smoke from the burning villages mixed with the black smoke that arose from the fuel and ammunition dumps that had been set ablaze with incendiary devices.

Faced with such a desperate situation, the majority view among Chiang's high command was that with Xuzhou effectively lost, the only realistic military course was to withdraw all Nationalist forces from the area so that they could regroup elsewhere. This would mean that the NRA would have suffered only a setback, not a major defeat. But Chiang, showing the stubbornness that he often confused with decisiveness, refused to accept that the whole Huaihai campaign was to be abandoned. He ordered that all NRA armies were to hold their ground and counter-attack where possible in order to distract the PLA's attention, while the Nationalist 13th Army fought its way out of Xuzhou.

General Du Yuming, who was now in command in Xuzhou, remained loyal to Chiang and prepared his troops, who were surviving on grass and animal bones, for one final attempt to break out. But events overtook him. On 6 January 1949 the PLA attacked Xuzhou on every front in a major tank, artillery and infantry offensive. Four days later the city fell. One hundred thousand NRA troops, including General Du, surrendered and were taken prisoner. The Nationalist 6th and 8th Armies, realizing the hopelessness of it all, had already given up their attempt to relieve Xuzhou.

It was the catastrophic defeat Mao had hoped for and Chiang had feared. All told, the Nationalists had lost a figure approaching 200,000 men, many of them the flower of Chiang's armies. His elite corps had been broken and a huge amount of equipment, the greater part being high-quality American weaponry, had fallen into Communist hands. Worse still for Chiang was that the Communists now controlled northern and central China. The way to the Nationalists' strongholds in

Nationalist casualties being airlifted from besieged Xuzhou in May 1948. (Photo by Popperfoto via Getty Images)

southern China now lay open. President Truman, who knew from Treasury figures that the USA had already provided the GMD with $2 billion in aid and $1 million in military hardware, told his State Department officials that Chiang was now a 'busted flush' who no longer deserved American aid.

What intensified the bitterness of the GMD's routing in the Huaihai campaign was that it coincided with the third great victory of the Communists in the winter of 1948/49 – success in the Pingjin campaign.

The Pingjin campaign, November 1948–January 1949

The speed of the PLA's triumph in the Liaoshen and Huaihai campaigns presented Mao with a problem. Should he immediately press on with his main objective – the destruction of Nationalist power in southern China – or should he pause to take Beijing and Tianjin, the two cities in northern China to which the GMD still clung? In strategic terms, there was no pressing need to occupy Beijing. Since the Communists now controlled northern China, Beijing offered no threat to them. It was merely a Nationalist pocket that would doubtless fall in time. However, a triumphalist note entered Mao's thinking. To seize Beijing, China's northern capital and central to the nation's history, would be of huge symbolic value, which would surely justify diverting troops to its capture even if it involved delaying the PLA's movement southwards.

For Mao, therefore, it was essentially a matter of prestige, but he was also exercised by the knowledge that, although Beijing was held by the Nationalists under their commander, Fu Zuoyi, there were a number of dissident movements within the city ready to challenge the GMD's authority. In July 1948, it had taken rifle fire to disperse a demonstration by 3,000 protesters. Mao wanted to take Beijing before such groups became a threat to the CCP's own authority.

It was such thinking that led him to order his commanders, Lin Biao and Nie Rongzhen, to undertake the Pingjin campaign, which took its name for the linking of the last syllables of Peiping, the Nationalist name for Beijing, and Tianjin, the main port on the gulf of the Yellow River and linked to the capital by the Grand Canal. The campaign, whose chronology overlapped the other two major campaigns, began in late November. Fu Zuoyi, the Nationalist commander in Beijing, also had a decision to make. Should he move his 350,000-strong army to assist the Nationalist forces who were under increasing pressure elsewhere in the north, or should he consolidate his position by drawing in the various GMD forces spread around the north China plain to tighten the Beijing–Tianjin line? Fu decided on the latter. It was the attempt to withdraw the GMD forces from Zhangjiakou, a town to the north-west of Beijing, that precipitated the first move in the campaign.

Learning of Fu Zuoyi's decision, Mao told Nie Rongzhen to link up with Lin Biao's forces and cut off the

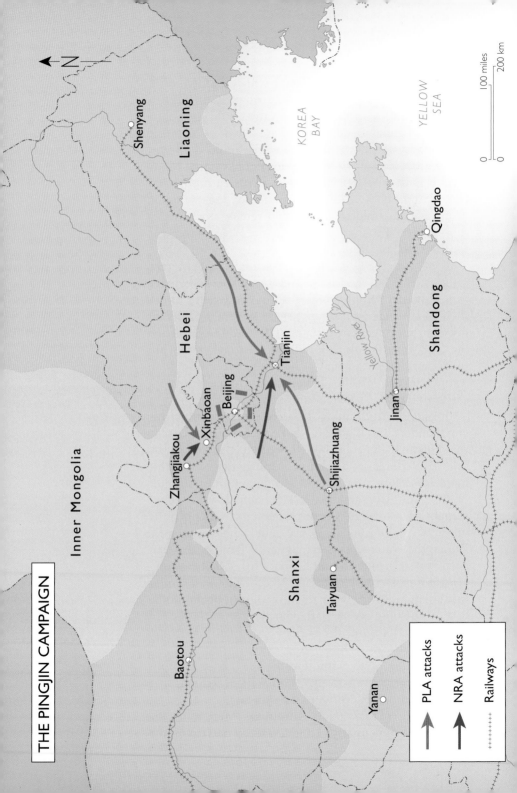

THE PINGJIN CAMPAIGN

N

Inner Mongolia

Liaoning

Shenyang

Hebei

KOREA BAY

YELLOW SEA

Zhangjiakou
Xinbaoan
Beijing
Tianjin

Qingdao

Shandong

Shijiazhuang

Jinan

Yellow River

Shanxi

Taiyuan

Baotou

Yanan

PLA attacks
NRA attacks
Railways

100 miles
200 km

Nationalist army as it moved south. The NRA columns found themselves ambushed at Xinbaoan, a town north of Beijing. In an attempt to save the entrapped units, Fu called on the NRA's 35th Army at Tianjin to come to their aid, but as the 35th approached Xinbaoan they too became caught between Nie's and Lin's attackers. In late December, sustained shellfire from a range of batteries pinned the defenders in the walled town, whose defences were steadily reduced to rubble. PLA infantry then poured through the gaps; a blood orgy followed as the troops went from street to street, house to house, killing those who continued to resist.

By the time the surrender finally came, Guo Jingyun, the NRA commander in Xinbaoan, had shot himself. In a macabre gesture the PLA, having first refrigerated Guo's corpse in the frozen ground, later sent it on to Beijing where it was publicly displayed as a terrifying intimation of what was likely to befall the inhabitants.

The fall of Xinbaoan sealed the fate of Zhangjiakou, which within two days had also been taken by the PLA, this time with little resistance shown by the defenders. Mao next targeted Tianjin, where the bulk of the NRA's armies were stationed. There was some delay before an attack was made, one reason being that the recent defeats had depressed Fu Zuoyi, to the point where he doubted that the Communists were now stoppable. He sent representatives to them suggesting a truce, hoping – fruitlessly as it turned out – that in the meantime Chiang and Mao would consider reopening peace talks.

A second reason for the delay was that Zhou Enlai put it to Mao that a heavy bombardment of Tianjin and Beijing risked irreparably damaging those cities' industrial and manufacturing plants, which if taken intact could greatly aid the CCP's war effort. Lin Biao also added to the case for avoiding battle over Pingjin by suggesting that it would serve the PLA's interests better if they were to conserve their forces and concentrate on taking southern China.

Although Mao gave thought to these arguments, in the end he kept to his original belief that the prestige value of taking Tianjin and Beijing outweighed all other considerations; the campaign would go on. Mao later told the Soviet Union that he had deliberately delayed the attack so as to give Chiang a chance to enter into negotiations. However, given that Mao was intent on taking Beijing and had made no serious effort to offer terms to the GMD, this explanation seems unlikely. Whatever the reasons for the delay, by 14 January 1949 it was all over. On that day, Lin Biao, in accordance with Mao's order, launched the assault on Tianjin. It was another bloody affair. The NRA troops under Chen Changjie, the Nationalist commander in the city, fought tenaciously and courageously through the day and into the night. But with no prospect of reinforcements coming to their assistance, there was little real chance they could hold on. On the dawn of 15 January, Chen Changjie told his men to lay down their arms. He then formally surrendered.

There was now nothing to prevent the PLA from taking Beijing. The only issue was whether the Nationalists would go down fighting to defend it. By the time Tianjin fell, PLA detachments had already occupied many of Beijing's outlying suburbs, meeting only token resistance. There was a strange atmosphere in the city itself. Everyone knew that carnage might soon follow but life seemed to go on as usual; packed trams rattled along, shops and cinemas stayed open, people went to work. There was not the desperate rush to leave that had produced the panic-stricken scenes in other threatened cities. It may have been this that helped persuade Fu Zuoyi to negotiate rather than fight. In truth, he needed little persuading. The talks he held with PLA spokesmen clearly indicated that the Communists were prepared to smash their way mercilessly into Beijing. The only alternative, they told him, was for all of his 200,000 troops to vacate the city. On 16 January Fu accepted the ultimatum and ordered his forces to prepare to leave. He added that he no longer recognized the authority of the Nationalist government in Nanjing to rule China.

On 31 January the Communist takeover of Beijing began. In a great triumphal display, thousands of troops

Nationalist forces manning a Japanese-made 155mm howitzer, part of the artillery defences ringing Shanghai in May 1949. (Photo by Popperfoto via Getty Images)

marched, rode or drove through the city. An American observer, Derk Bodde, noted that the procession took an hour to pass him. He counted over 250 heavy motor vehicles of every type: 'tanks, armoured cars, truckloads of soldiers, trucks mounted with machine guns, trucks towing heavy artillery, innumerable ambulances, jeeps, and other smaller vehicles'. Bodde believed he was witnessing 'probably the greatest demonstration of Chinese military might in history'. What amazed him was that it was 'primarily a display of *American* military equipment, virtually all of it captured or obtained from Guomindang sources'.

The taking of Beijing by the PLA marked the climax of a remarkable period. In scarcely more than four months the Communists had won three overwhelming victories. They had driven the GMD from northern China and were now poised to extend their authority over the whole of the country. In a dramatic reaction, Chiang Kai-shek acknowledged his responsibility for the Nationalists' humiliation by resigning. In Nanjing on 21 January, knowing that Beijing had fallen – a loss that confirmed the failure of the Nationalist strategy he had insisted on – he handed over authority to Li Zongren, his vice-president.

Yet while Chiang had honoured the Chinese tradition of performing self-abasement following failure, it had been only a gesture. He did not genuinely intend giving up his power within the Guomindang. This could be read between the lines of his resignation statement in which he declared that Li Zongren 'will act for me', a clear indication that Chiang still regarded himself as retaining the ultimate authority in the party. In all his subsequent actions he behaved as before. He kept the title Generalissimo and continued to consult and direct the GMD's military commanders as if he were their leader, behaviour that they reciprocated by treating him as their chief.

The final struggles, 1949

Following the Pingjin campaign, the remainder of the war had an air of inevitability about it. Fierce struggles still took place, but at best the Nationalists were engaged in delaying actions. Chiang Kai-shek continued to urge his forces to defend their remaining positions on the mainland, but it was clear he no longer believed that the Communists could be prevented from taking the whole of China. What followed was, in effect, a slow surrender. Since both the USA and the Soviet Union had now rejected any notion that they might come directly to the GMD's aid, Chiang's thoughts turned to Taiwan, a large island 90 miles from the mainland, as a refuge from which he could rebuild his party and his own power.

The Nationalist experience in Taiwan had so far been a turbulent one. Having been under Japanese colonial rule since 1895, the Taiwanese had regarded the Nationalists' arrogant reclaiming of the island in 1945 as the replacement of one oppressive regime by another. They deeply resented being treated as if they had been collaborators. Under direct instruction from Chiang, the NRA forces violently ousted the local people from their houses, shops and businesses, and denied them any say in government. In frustration, the Taiwanese in February 1947 mounted a large-scale demonstration in Taipei,

OPPOSITE
Li Zongren took over as GMD leader after Chiang gave up defending the mainland in 1949.
(Philip Jowett)

贊襄偉業規模遠達

副總統姓李，名宗仁，字德鄰。清光緒十七年辛卯一八九一年生於廣西臨桂縣。西陸軍速成學校畢業。曾參加反袁世凱帝制及護法各役。民國十一年率所部回廣西擊破陸榮廷等舊桂系軍隊。十五年國民革命軍北伐，就任國民革命軍第七軍軍長，分會主席。民國十六年國民政府定都南京，李氏率第七軍平定武漢政府，任武漢政治分會主席。十八年蔣李分裂，李氏自治兩湖，與中央軍同行三角之戰。民國二十年就任廣西省政府主席，努力於地方自治，及省政建設，樹立廣西模範省之稱。抗戰軍興，任第五戰區司令長官，徐州會戰，先後殲日本板垣、磯谷兩師團，獲得臺兒莊勝利，戰績彪炳，為現代軍事家。由民國二十年起任國民政府委員，廿五年起任國民黨中央監察委員。卅七年四月，在第一屆國民代表大會當選為行憲第一任副總統。

the island's capital, only for it to be crushed bloodily by the Nationalist forces, who killed over 10,000 of the protestors. Now, with the physical resistance of the islanders broken, Taiwan became an obvious haven and base for the Nationalists in the increasingly likely event of their being defeated on the mainland.

While Chiang prepared to reconstruct his regime in Taiwan, he left to Li Zongren the unenviable task of defending the indefensible on the mainland. Chiang wanted such Nationalist cities as Nanjing and Shanghai to hold out for as long as possible, not because he believed they could be permanently saved, but because he wanted time to transfer as many financial and material assets as possible from those cities to Taiwan. For similar reasons he refused to send reinforcements to Nanjing – he wanted to transfer GMD armies intact to Taiwan.

Nanjing fell in April 1949 and Shanghai a month later. Before their fall the Nationalist cities became chaotic and violent places. In Nanjing, looting was commonplace as ordinary people, desperate for anything they could lay their hands on, sacked the premises vacated by self-serving officials, who tried to commandeer the last transports to leave the city. Sometimes the police brutally attacked the looters; sometimes they joined them. Before they left Shanghai, wealthy Nationalists transferred millions of dollars' worth of gold and silver bullion to Taiwan. In a desperate bid to hold on to Shanghai, the city's fanatical Nationalist governor, Tang Enbo, ordered execution squads to operate on a daily basis. In scenes reminiscent of Berlin in the last months of World War II in Europe, gangs of soldiers went round executing inhabitants who dared suggest that the fight against the CCP was a lost cause.

Yet such murderous zeal was not matched at the higher levels of the GMD's command. Too many of Chiang's military had resigned themselves to eventual defeat. This did not stop others continuing to show commitment, but the organized leadership that was required if the Nationalists were to save any part of mainland China never materialized. Chiang continued

OPPOSITE
In an attempt to prevent disorder spreading in besieged Shanghai, police rounded up desperate homeless women, many with children, and sent them to relief shelters. (Bettmann/ Getty Images)

Shanghai witnessed a reign of terror before it fell in May 1949. It was a common sight for suspected Communist sympathisers to be executed in the street. (Philip Jowett)

to issue orders but, since these often conflicted with those given by Li Zongren, the result was uncertainty and bewilderment among the defenders. Li said in exasperation that he wished Chiang would either take over full command or leave mainland China. When Chiang, who had come to Shanghai as a last gesture of resolve, realized the imminent PLA onslaught would be unstoppable, he slipped away and sailed for Taiwan for temporary respite. The taking of the city involved relatively little fighting. There were pockets of resistance but since Mao, keen to conserve his forces, made no great effort to cut off the fleeing troops who rushed from Shanghai, casualties were light compared to the bloodletting that had occurred in other cities.

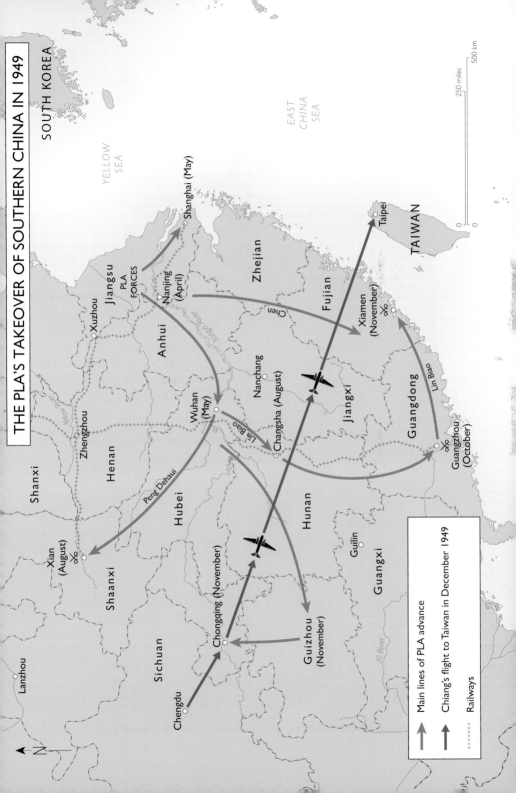

THE PLA'S TAKEOVER OF SOUTHERN CHINA IN 1949

SOUTH KOREA

YELLOW SEA

EAST CHINA SEA

Shanghai (May)

Jiangsu

PLA FORCES

Xuzhou

Nanjing (April)

Anhui

Zhejian

Fujian

TAIWAN

Taipei

Chen

Zhengzhou

Henan

Wuhan (May)

Yangzi River

Nanchang

Changsha (August)

Jiangxi

Xiamen (November)

Shanxi

Shaanxi

Xian (August)

Peng Dehuai

Lin Biao

Hunan

Guangdong

Lin Biao

Guangzhou (October)

Hubei

Chongqing (November)

Guizhou (November)

Guilin

Guangxi

Lanzhou

Sichuan

Chengdu

Xi River

Main lines of PLA advance

Chiang's flight to Taiwan in December 1949

Railways

500 km

250 miles

N

The fall of Nanjing and Shanghai coincided with another of the great symbolic events of the Civil War, the crossing of the Yangzi by the Communists. In Chinese tradition the Yangzi, the nation's greatest river, was a life source. Moreover, for the Communists to control it meant that it was no longer the physical barrier that had hitherto defined the extent of their power. So significant was it as a symbol that some Nationalists had suggested it should be treated as a moat guarding the entrance to southern China, which had always been where the GMD's greatest strength lay. Therefore, ran the argument, the PLA's crossing should be prevented at all costs. Yet in the event, the Nationalist resistance melted away. Deng Xiaoping expressed his surprise: 'We did not encounter fierce resistance anywhere. Nearly all our 300,000 men crossed the river in a 24-hour period, plunging the enemy troops into chaos – they fled helter skelter.'

It was the Chinese Communists' control of the Yangzi that led to Britain's being directly caught up in the Civil War, in what became known as the Yangzi

Nationalist troops surrendering to the PLA during the battle for Shanghai, May 1949. (Photo by Keystone/Hulton Archive/Getty Images)

incident. On 20 April 1949, a PLA mortar battery on the north bank of the Yangzi opened fire on HMS *Amethyst*, a British warship en route from Shanghai to Nanjing to give protection to the British Embassy there. The shelling killed 16 of the crew and caused the ship to run aground. After it attempted to return fire, *Amethyst*'s guns were knocked out of action. A British frigate tried to come to its assistance but it, too, was fired upon. After 100 days, during which the *Amethyst* sat with PLA guns trained on it, the ship was able to slip away in July and make the 100-mile journey downriver to safety. The UK press described the affair as a final triumph, since despite the overall number of deaths on the British vessels rising to 50, the ship's captain had defied the PLA's demand that he apologize for violating Chinese waters. However, there was little doubt that the Chinese Communists had shown restraint. Given the position of the *Amethyst,* it would have been blown out of the water had the PLA batteries been ordered to continue their shelling.

After the Yangzi had been crossed, key GMD bases continued to fall regularly to the PLA as it pushed into the southern provinces; Changsha fell in August, and Ghangzhou in October. It was on 1 October that Mao publicly declared that the Civil War had been won. On the balcony of the Forbidden City in Beijing, he announced to the world that 'China has stood up' and that a new nation, the Communist People's Republic of China, had come into being. His confidence was justified; although resistance continued, there was now no possibility of the Nationalist regime surviving on the mainland. As ever, the character of the resistance depended on the dedication and determination of the resistors, and particularly on how well they were led. A recurrent problem in the last months of the war was the tension between Li Zongren and Chiang. So divided were the two men that they deliberately avoided contact and correspondence. There were even suggestions among some of the embittered NRA generals that Chiang should be arrested and held in custody to prevent him from causing disruption.

勝利渡長江

The Nationalists made a last stand in Chongqing, which they declared was now the nation's capital – as it had been in the final years of the Japanese war. As had occurred in Nanjing and Shanghai, the Nationalist defenders often fought viciously among themselves as the Communist forces approached. Chiang Kai-shek went in person to Chongqing in an effort to rally the troops there, but he did not stay long. When he realized that, with Deng Xiaoping's forces poised to attack, the position was hopeless, he fled to Chengdu only to find that that city, too, was about to be attacked. On 10 December, Chiang fled by plane from Chengdu to Taiwan. He was never to set foot on mainland China again. Sporadic fighting continued, but the PLA was now engaged in what was essentially a series of mopping-up operations. Although no formal end to the war was ever declared, if any one event can be said to have marked the end of the Chinese Civil War it was Chiang Kai-shek's flight to Taiwan.

Western China

Chiang and the Nationalists faced a perennial ethnic and religious problem in China's most westerly states, Tibet and Xinjiang, which were areas larger in size than Western Europe. In Tibet, the great majority of the population were adherents of the Lama faith, a branch of Buddhism. In Xinjiang most were Muslims. The Tibetans were ethnically and culturally distinct from the Han race, which made up 90 per cent of the population of China. Equally different from the Han were the Uighur, Kazakh, Hui and Kirghiz races of Xinjiang. Neither of the two warring sides in the Civil War was welcome in these two western states but it was Chiang who had the greater problem. A Xinjiang resistance movement developed, which Chiang pacified to some extent by promising some degree of local autonomy. Nevertheless, such was the concern that the province could flare up at any time that 100,000 Nationalist troops were stationed there throughout the Civil War. Similar tensions existed

A CCP propaganda poster celebrates Mao's taking of the salute in Tiananmen Square after his announcement of the creation of the People's Republic of China in October 1949. (Philip Jowett)

between Chiang's government and Tibet, and although any military threat to the Nationalists from the region was minimal, the presence of alienated peoples in the west was a constant reminder of how fractured Chiang Kai-shek's hold over China was.

The position was to be violently resolved after Chiang had been defeated. In 1950, the armies of what was now the People's Republic of China undertook a series of carefully planned 'pacification' campaigns, which broke the meagre military resistance that Tibet and Xinjiang could muster and imposed Communist control. Yet over seventy years later the separatist movements within the two provinces still presented a challenge to Beijing's authority. The desire among Tibetans for independence has not been crushed, despite Beijing's ongoing attempt to destroy their language traditions and culture. Xinjiang tells a similarly grim story. Unwilling to accept Muslim Uighur demands for independence, PRC governments from Mao to the present have continued to employ the most repressive means to enforce Communist conformity.

THE GREAT PROTAGONISTS
Chiang Kai-shek and Mao Zedong

Mao Zedong's record up to 1949 was a truly remarkable one. He had led a vast social revolution, had defeated the Japanese invaders and the Nationalists, and had created the People's Republic of China, the world's largest Communist state. Set against these successes, Chiang Kai-shek's record seemed barren. Having been the dominant force in China for over a decade, he lost the Civil War and was driven from the mainland. It would be easy, therefore, to see Chiang's career up to this point as a failure. But that would be to overlook his very considerable achievements. Before his defeat in 1949, Chiang had become the embodiment of the Chinese nation, his name being recognized worldwide in a way that no previous Chinese leader had achieved. He had been the first modern Chinese statesman to come anywhere near establishing his country as an independent sovereign nation with a renewed sense of its own identity and the potential to become a world power.

Refusing to accept the legitimacy of the Communist control of the mainland, Chiang and succeeding GMD governments continued to claim to represent the true China. Some of Chiang's apologists have pushed his claims much further. They argue that he was the first true modernizer of China, who was prevented from achieving his final goal of forging a united people and nation only by the invasion of the Japanese and the opposition of the Communist rebels. Mao and the CCP stole the victory that belonged rightly to Chiang. Other commentators are more critical; they suggest that Chiang was and remained essentially a warlord who, having risen to the top of the GMD by ruthless military means, intrigued and plotted with some of the worst elements in Chinese society in order to sustain himself in power. His reliance on devious and corrupt Chinese and foreign financiers effectively prevented him from ever truly representing the Chinese people and rendered him incapable of pursuing the social transformation that originally inspired Sun Yatsen's Guomindang.

It is true that Chiang always spoke in terms of his party and government leading a moral revolution. In 1934 he had launched a 'New Life Movement', intended as a rejection of both Communism and Western capitalism and a reassertion of Chinese values of social harmony. But the narrow basis of his financial and political support and the demands of constant war meant he was very restricted in what he could do. This was particularly evident in the GMD's economic dealings in which, despite Chiang's supposed strictures, it took capitalism as the model – a decision that necessarily meant close and continuing association with Western commercial and financial interests.

Mao and Chiang came from similar social backgrounds. They were the sons of well-to-do peasant families. Both had been forced into arranged marriages that they refused to consummate and later rejected. Both had proved rebellious pupils and students. They also shared many personal characteristics. Both were hypochondriacs. When under stress, both showed signs of psychosomatic disorder: Chiang suffered recurrent nosebleeds, while Mao was chronically constipated and periodically gave way to bouts of depression. Neither man was easy to get on with. Though they had many acquaintances, it is unlikely that either ever had close friends. Each had a strong puritanical streak. Where they differed was that Mao's puritanism was a thing of his youth, Chiang's of his adulthood. As if to make up

OPPOSITE
Chiang reviews his troops after establishing the Nationalist regime in Taiwan following his flight from the mainland in 1949. (Photo by Central Press/Hulton Archive/Getty Images)

for his former abstinence as a young man when he had regarded women as a distraction from the important things in life, Mao in his later years become a libertine. Chiang went in a reverse direction. Mortified by the discovery at the time of his second marriage in 1921 that he had unwittingly infected his new wife with the gonorrhoea he had contracted in a drunken orgy in a Shanghai brothel, he vowed to abstain from alcohol and extra-marital sex, a promise that he seems largely to have honoured, though he continued to have platonic affairs with other women.

As their conduct during the Civil War illustrated, both Mao and Chiang were ruthless, but no leader in 20th-century China could have afforded to be anything else. The lack of any mechanism in Chinese politics for the peaceable transference of power meant that violent struggle was the norm. Unless a claimant was prepared to be violent he could not gain or retain real authority. That was a basic truth in Chinese politics that both Mao and Chiang acknowledged and acted upon. Neither was above using strong-arm tactics, even torture in Mao's case. When suppressing a mutiny in the Red Army Mao had instructed his officers: 'Do not kill the important leaders too quickly, but squeeze the information out of them. From the clues they give, you can go on to unearth other leaders.'

How careless Chiang could be with the lives of civilians was clear in his decision to re-route the Yellow River in 1947. This massive dam project, aimed at dividing the CCP forces from their bases on the northern bank, resulted in half a million people in some 600 villages being uprooted and left homeless. Chiang laid himself further open to the charge that he was not genuinely interested in democracy by the way in which he hounded the Democratic League, a party set up in 1939 to offer a third way between the Nationalists and Communists and help unite China against the Japanese. Despite the League's conciliatory approach, Chiang declined to consider any form of merger unless the League subordinated itself totally to the Guomindang.

OPPOSITE
Chiang and Meiling Soong after taking up residence in Taiwan in 1950. Meiling's charm and vivacity contributed greatly to Chiang's advancement in Chinese and international affairs. (Bettmann/Getty Images)

There were suggestions that he was implicated in the assassination in 1946 of two of the League's leading figures, Wen Yiduo and Li Gongpu. Although the rumours were never substantiated, the murders provided the Communists with a useful propaganda weapon to use against Chiang and the GMD.

The suffering that Chiang presided over was more a consequence of culpable neglect – as with the wretched treatment meted out to recruits to the NRA – than of planned brutality. Of course, huge numbers died during the Civil War and charges could be levelled against both leaders that their strategies were responsible for the deaths of millions. But that in itself does not prove that Mao and Chiang willed those fatalities. What can be said is that the two men exhibited the indifference to people's suffering that was habitual among Chinese leaders.

While it is appropriate to describe Mao Zedong as a Chinese Marxist, the stress should be on the adjective rather than the noun. Throughout his political career Mao's first objective was the furtherance of the interests of China, not the pursuit of international revolution. Indeed, one of his major political achievements was to redefine and restructure Marxist theory to make it fit the Chinese context. Mao once said in his earthy, peasant way that only the Chinese 'with their arses planted firmly in the soil of their native land' could truly understand China. His determination that the Chinese people must follow their own path was a reaction against the Soviet Union's attempt to dictate to the CCP.

It is noteworthy how little practical experience Mao had of international relations. True, he was widely read in translated foreign works, but, aged 52 in 1945, he had never been out of China and thus had none of the real knowledge of the world that marked the cosmopolitan Zhou Enlai, his ablest colleague and future foreign minister. Chiang in contrast had lived in Japan and Russia and, through his third wife, Soong Meiling, whom he wed in 1927, was increasingly introduced to Western ways. Meiling, who had graduated from an American university and was the sister of the financier

OPPOSITE
Mao and his third wife, Jiang Qing, in 1946. Their tempestuous marriage survived until Mao's death in 1976. (Photo by: Universal History Archive/UIG via Getty Images)

T.V. Soong, China's richest man, became for Chiang what might be called an indispensable liability. Chiang knew only a few English words and was dependent on her when negotiating with the Western allies. He could not do without Meiling but she occasioned great scandal. Beautiful and highly intelligent, she used her charms to great effect and turned heads wherever she went. She often acted as Chiang's representative and there is little doubt that the Western press fell in love with her. She was said to have seduced many members of the American delegations in China, all in the cause of advancing her husband's career. Obsessively fastidious, Meiling would never sleep twice in the same set of bedsheets and insisted on gold taps being fitted in her bathrooms.

Interestingly, their marriage produced no children. It was rumoured that this was because Chiang, having sired a son with a previous wife, made it a condition of marrying Meiling that their relationship would be a celibate one. They preferred playing croquet or draughts together or listening to American big band records on a wind-up gramophone. This homely picture sits oddly with Chiang's reputation as someone who had previously enjoyed several affairs. But his womanizing aside, Chiang had few other personal vices. Indeed, the irony of his leadership was that, while his government and party became associated with corruption and excess, he personally led an upright life in accordance with his own brand of ascetic Christianity and Buddhism.

Arguably, the only woman on whom Mao ever depended was his mother, a saintly long-suffering Buddhist. It is true he wrote love poems of some poignancy to his second wife, but this did not stop him abandoning her and taking a third wife, Jiang Qing, whom he came to loathe but for some reason never abandoned. Jiang later proved a formidable figure in Chinese politics. But although Jiang's prominence as Mao's wife seemed to confirm the CCP's official recognition of female equality, in practice women were seldom treated as equals in the party.

The Chinese have been described as natural dialecticians, believers that life is essentially a struggle between opposites. Both Chiang and Mao were firm in their conviction that compromise was not a solution to any of China's major problems. Complete victory over opponents was the only option, both politically and militarily. The upbringing of the two antagonists was very similar. They had grown up in a China rent by crisis and upheaval, where strength was admired and weakness despised. The violence that was a constant feature of Chinese history was not an accidental accompaniment to political action; it was a definition of what politics was. At its most basic, politics in 20th-century China was a matter of one claimant for power trying to destroy all elements of opposition. Absent was any democratic notion of legitimate opposition or government by consent. Whatever the subtleties of the ideas they separately espoused, Chiang and Mao each acted on the belief that ultimately force was the only arbiter in public affairs, hence the savagery of the Civil War of 1946–49.

Since the dates of the Chinese Civil War coincided with the first years of the Cold War, there is an understandable tendency to see it as a microcosm of that larger international struggle. However, it was never a simple matter of the Soviet-backed Communists versus the American-backed Nationalists. The relationship of the Chinese parties with the two major powers was a more complex affair.

The Soviet Union and China

Mao regarded Stalin's policies towards China as being deliberately devious. He had strong grounds for thinking so. At the end of the Pacific War, Stalin, rather than assisting the CCP in seizing the territory now relinquished by the Japanese, had allowed thousands of Nationalist troops to pour into Manchuria. This had been under the terms of the Sino-Soviet Treaty of Friendship agreed with Chiang's GMD government in August 1945. Chiang's hope was that the alliance with the Soviet Union would give him a free hand to crush the Chinese Communists. For his part, Stalin wanted Manchuria's industrial resources. Stalin went on to urge Mao to show restraint and to enter into talks with Chiang Kai-shek. Since this was what the USA was also advocating, Mao reluctantly agreed. Even after the GMD–CCP talks had broken down, Stalin still declined to commit himself unequivocally to the Chinese Communists. Early in 1946, much to Mao's annoyance, the Soviet Union announced that it still desired 'to assist the Nationalist government to establish its power in the north-east'.

However, Stalin then made a shift of policy. Both as a sop to Mao and as a way of preventing the Nationalists from fully controlling Manchuria, he instructed the local Soviet commanders to hand over to the CCP forces large numbers of weapons captured from the Japanese. But then, in another policy zigzag, Stalin commanded the Chinese Communists to abandon the territory they had taken in northern China. To enforce this demand, Soviet commanders in China threatened to turn their weapons against those CCP detachments that refused to obey. Peng Zheng, one of Mao's divisional officers, commented on the bitter irony of 'the army of one Communist party using tanks to drive out the army of another!' The Chinese Communists were understandably often bewildered by Soviet conduct. They were as likely to be turned on as enemies as they were to be treated as Marxist allies.

Stalin's attitude towards the Civil War derived from his belief that it was neither possible nor desirable for Mao's

Stalin looks on as Molotov signs the Treaty of Friendship between the Soviet Union and Chiang's Chinese Republic, 14 August 1945. (Bettmann/Getty Images)

Communists to control the whole of China. In April 1948, he was still urging Mao's CCP to enter a coalition and not attempt to govern on its own. He appealed to Mao to think in terms of a 'national revolutionary-democratic government, rather than a Communist one'. Mao rejected the notion. Yet Stalin persisted. When Chiang, faced by the disastrous reverses that his armies were suffering in the autumn campaigns of 1948, asked both America and the USSR to renew their roles as peace brokers, Stalin suggested that Mao should be prepared to consider a CCP–GMD settlement.

Again, Mao declined to listen. In a 1949 New Year's Day broadcast, he dismissed Chiang and the GMD as 'snake-like scoundrels who deserved no pity'. In a telegram to Stalin, he told him that the war was running 'irreversibly' in the CCP's favour and that by the summer the PLA would be in a position to cross the Yangzi and take the war into southern China. In April 1949, as the PLA forces prepared to make Mao's prophecy a reality, Stalin again interfered. He sought to frighten Mao by suggesting that if the PLA did cross the Yangzi this might well excite intervention by the Americans, who would not tolerate a China totally controlled by the Communists. Stalin proposed that Mao accept the partitioning of China along the Yangzi, which would leave a Communist north and a Nationalist south. Mao, however, once more refused to be instructed. He judged that Stalin was primarily concerned not with the USA's reaction but with preventing a united Communist China from rivalling the Soviet Union. Mao later recorded: 'When we were about to cross the Yangzi River, Stalin still wanted to prevent us. According to him, if we did so, America would send troops to China. I did not listen to what he said. We crossed the Yangzi. America did not send troops.'

Ambiguous as it appeared, there was an underlying consistency in Stalin's approach to the Chinese Civil War. As Mao had correctly sensed, Stalin's abiding concern was to keep China divided. A China ineffectively controlled by Chiang Kai-shek and the Nationalists

ПУСТЬ ЖИВЁТ И КРЕПНЕТ
НЕРУШИМАЯ ДРУЖБА И СОТРУДНИЧЕСТВО
СОВЕТСКОГО И КИТАЙСКОГО НАРОДОВ!

A Soviet propaganda poster entitled 'Long live indestructible friendship and cooperation', suggesting mutual respect between the Communist leaders. In reality, the two men did not trust each other. (Album / Alamy Stock Photo)

was far more to Stalin's taste than a committed, united Communist China under Mao Zedong. It chimed with his preference for a weak, unchallenging state as a Far Eastern neighbour. Preoccupied as he became with Cold War machinations in Europe, the last thing Stalin wanted was a resurgent and threatening China on the Soviet Union's 4,000-mile Asian border.

Stalin's attitude was also shaped by major ideological considerations. He was disturbed by the thought that if the CCP triumphed, Mao's China might well come to challenge the Soviet Union's leadership of international Communism. Differences over the meaning of Marxism and how it should be applied in China had bedevilled relations between Mao and Stalin since the 1920s. They had not acted in a spirit of Communist brotherhood. Stalin had been unwilling to accept that a peasant-based movement such as Mao was leading could be genuinely revolutionary. The Marxist rules of class war as interpreted by the Kremlin dictated that true proletarian revolution had to be urban based. Although Stalin was quite prepared to ignore Marxist dialectics when they did not fit the Soviet situation, he was rigidly dogmatic when applying them outside the USSR. This long-standing ideological rivalry was intensified by the mutual distaste the Soviet and Chinese leaders felt towards each other. Stalin much preferred negotiating with Chiang than with Mao, whom he considered an opinionated upstart.

China and the USA

In the 1950s, there was much recrimination among Americans over what was termed the 'loss' of China. The charge was that the USA, despite having invested heavily in time, diplomacy and resources in China, had allowed it to fall to Communism. Stalin, the argument ran, had outmanoeuvred the USA and, using Mao as a puppet, had established China as a Soviet satellite in Asia. The creation of the PRC was thus one of Stalin's great Cold War triumphs. Mao's Soviet-backed victory had helped bring into being a vast Communist empire reaching from Eastern Europe to the Pacific. It is understandable why in the febrile atmosphere of the McCarthy era in the USA such an interpretation should have taken hold. But it is a view that few analysts would now accept. We now know that Mao was far from being Stalin's puppet and that Stalin had no wish to see China become a powerful Communist state.

The attitude of the US officials in China in 1945 had been far from hostile towards the CCP. This was because the Communists, like the GMD, had been allies of the Americans since 1941 and also because

Mao deliberately played down the CCP's politics. He stressed to the Americans that his party were agrarian reformers rather than political revolutionaries. This may have been a temporary expedient, but it certainly made many Americans feel well disposed towards the CCP at this stage. This respect was increased when Mao put forward a plan for a CCP–GMD coalition government to run China once Japan had been defeated. Negotiations followed over a number of months, with Patrick Hurley, the extrovert US ambassador, giving his full support. When the talks collapsed in March 1945 it was largely Chiang Kai-shek's fault; he let it be known that he was not prepared to accord the CCP parity with his own party.

The reaction this caused among the Americans revealed how seriously divided they were on the China issue. While Hurley would not openly criticize Chiang, a number of US officials were more candid. In reporting to the State Department, they referred back to the withering comments made in 1943 by General Stillwell, Chiang's American chief of staff. Stillwell had condemned the GMD as being chronically guilty of 'corruption, neglect, hoarding, black market, trading with the enemy'. Equally pertinently, Stillwell and his successor, General Wedemeyer, described the CCP as a genuine social and political force in China, one that could not, therefore, be left out of any settlement. It was such thinking that led to George Marshall's appointment as President Truman's special China envoy in December 1945, in the hope that he could broker a GMD–CCP settlement.

Interestingly, while in China, Marshall took time to visit the Communist base at Yanan. Mao was careful to put on a good display, endeavouring to convince the Americans that the CCP were not rebels intent on overthrowing Chiang's legitimate government of China, but reformers concerned to improve the conditions of China's rural poor. The Communists were, Mao said, willing to co-operate in a joint Chinese venture, but it was the Nationalists who put barriers in the way. Marshall was sufficiently convinced by this line to report back favourably to Washington on the CCP's intentions. It also encouraged him to act tough with the Nationalists. On a number of occasions, Marshall used the threat of withholding supplies to the GMD to oblige Chiang to accept at least a temporary halt in the fighting. This tended to favour the Communists since they used the intermissions to strengthen the positions they held. Yet, in the end, Marshall's efforts to secure a settlement foundered when he realised that he could not convince Chiang of the need for a compromise.

Manifestly, the USA had expended much goodwill and great diplomatic energy in China in the aftermath of the Japanese war. However, it is doubtful that the Americans would have stayed as long as they did in China after 1945 had the Cold War not imposed the USA's larger concerns. It was the Americans' worry over how Stalin might use their absence to Soviet advantage that gave them pause and put back their formal withdrawal to 1947. That is why, exasperated with Chiang though they were, they never formally abandoned him, despite finally withdrawing their mission early in 1947. The Communists played on the continued American presence after the Pacific War had ended to suggest that Chiang Kai-shek was willing to sacrifice China's independence simply to shore up his own position. For his part, Chiang was never entirely happy with his reliance on the USA. He would have liked to continue playing off the Russians and the Americans against each other indefinitely.

It was also the case that, whatever the USA's official intentions may have been, its continued presence in China after 1945 damaged its reputation. Rather than creating stability, the presence of American forces in places such as Beijing, Shanghai and Tianjin sometimes made things worse. GIs were accused of arrogantly disregarding Chinese sensibilities in their dealings with locals. Furthermore, charges were made that they molested females; a particular incident that caused outrage among the Chinese in 1946 was the alleged rape of a young woman in Beijing by two US Marines. In July 1946, a motor column of American Marines was ambushed by a Communist detachment outside Beijing.

President Truman had a poor opinion of Chiang Kai-shek, but he never entirely abandoned the Nationalists. This was in part because of pressure from the Republican pro-Nationalist lobby in the US Congress. (Bettmann/Getty Images)

In the ensuing gun battle, four Marines were killed and 12 others wounded. Despite strong diplomatic protests from the USA, little co-operation was offered by the local people and Chiang was unable to flush out the Communists thought to be responsible. It was such incidents and the failure to persuade the two Chinese sides to compromise that undermined any real hope that the USA could achieve its ends in China.

Despite the harsh criticisms of the GMD regime by many American experts in the field, it is not difficult to grasp why the USA persisted in supporting Chiang Kai-shek and the Nationalists. By 1946, the USA had already committed huge resources to shoring up the GMD. Under a lend–lease scheme it had issued millions of dollars' worth of military equipment to the Nationalists. It had provided transport to carry over half a million GMD troops to the zones surrendered by the Japanese, an operation described by one American general as 'the greatest air and sea transportation in history'. In addition, 55,000 US Marines had been sent to the northern ports as 'military advisers' to the GMD. The USA judged that such an outlay made it impossible simply to write off its political and economic investment. The result was that it continued to finance and support Chiang and the Nationalists, despite the deep differences of opinion within the US government over this.

President Truman never held a high opinion of Chiang and the Nationalists, describing them as 'grafters and crooks'. In 1948, he pointedly declined to come to Chiang's aid when the GMD leader appealed for direct assistance against the Communist advance. Indeed, Truman would have willingly washed his hands of the Nationalists. However, Cold War concerns again intervened. In Congress, the hardening of the Cold War produced a vocal China lobby, largely made up of Republicans, which argued strongly that the Nationalists – whatever their failings – were an Asian bastion against the spread of international Communism and, therefore, could not be deserted.

The curious outcome of all this was that when the Chinese Communists won the Civil War in 1949 it was to the dismay of both of the two great powers. Mao's triumph confounded both the USA and the Soviet Union; it showed that Stalin had been wrong to underestimate the strength and durability of Chinese Communism and it indicated that the USA had been equally wrong to swallow its doubts about Chiang and commit itself to the support of the Nationalists. Both powers were left with the problem of trying to make the best of it. For two decades after 1949, the USA ignored political reality and pretended that Chiang's tiny island regime in Taiwan was the true Chinese nation, entitled even to take its seat as a permanent member of the UN Security Council. Forced by circumstance to acknowledge the PRC and publicly support it, since in Cold War terms it shared a common ideology, the Soviet Union under Stalin compensated by adopting a patronizing and exploitative approach towards Mao's China. This created a lasting bitterness among the Chinese that prevented there ever being a genuine partnership between the two Communist superpowers. Arguably, this division was one of the most significant factors in the ultimate victory of the West in the Cold War.

WHY THE WAR WAS WON AND LOST
GMD weakness – CCP strength

Given the GMD's superiority in 1946 in military resources, the Civil War was Chiang's to lose rather than Mao's to win. Although the struggle was often complex in its local detail, the overall story was relatively simple. It was essentially a matter of the CCP resisting the GMD's initial move to crush it and then taking the offensive. The major and deciding campaigns came after the GMD had been prevented from taking Manchuria and the north-east. This raises the very interesting question of whether Chiang sowed the seeds of his own defeat by following the wrong strategy.

Chiang's inability to maintain supplies to his forces in sufficient quantity exposed the mistake he had made in sending his major armies to Manchuria. In attempting to take the region, he had ignored the fears of those of his military advisers who had warned him that to proceed with the plan would be to overextend his supply lines and make his forces vulnerable to counter-attack in a region of China that was both hostile and relatively unknown to the Nationalists.

Chiang was too eager to extend his control over the whole of China. Retrospect suggests that he would have had a far better chance of spreading his authority had he first consolidated his position in central and southern China, where his real strength lay, before moving north. By abandoning the controlled methods he had employed against the Japanese and rushing to defeat the CCP in Manchuria, he threw away an advantage that his greater troop numbers and resources initially gave him. Chiang's lack of strategic judgement was further evident in his decision in 1947 to pursue the ironically misnamed 'strongpoint offensive'; intended to secure the north-eastern provinces for the GMD, it succeeded only in overstretching his armies at a time when they should have been regrouping and consolidating.

As the war progressed, the rivalry and jealousy among Chiang's generals proved to be a major weakness in the Nationalist army. Chiang also had a dangerous habit of appointing commanders according to their personal loyalty to him rather than their ability. More serious still was the readiness of key officers to act as Communist spies, leaking to the CCP details of Nationalist troop positions and movements.

With remarkable honesty and insight, Chiang himself in the last year of the war explained why his forces were losing to the enemy. He gave four principal reasons for this, the first being his military leaders' lack of tactical skill: 'Our commanders fight muddle-headed battles,' he said. He complained that they failed to study the opposing troop dispositions and took no account of the lie of the land. Their pre-planning was sketchy and they issued orders casually and thoughtlessly.

His second reason was the poor treatment the rank and file received from their officers. The troops were inadequately trained; their knowledge of weapon use was sketchy and they were not taught the rudiments of reconnoitring, manoeuvring, and maintaining lines of communication in the field. 'The soldiers' combat skills are so poor that they cannot fight', Chiang observed.

Chiang's third admission was that Nationalist morale was cripplingly low. 'It cannot be denied that the spirit of most commanders is broken and their morality is base,' he said. He also noted the complacency of the high-level officers, many of whom had lost their revolutionary spirit and were concerned solely with self-interest.

Chiang levelled his fourth and arguably weightiest self-reproach against the GMD itself as a political organization. Its work, he said, was done 'carelessly and perfunctorily'; the party lacked organization, discipline and effective propaganda, attributes in which, he acknowledged, Mao and the Communists excelled.

In a later reflection in the 1950s, Chiang Kai-shek added a fifth factor to explain his defeat. He emphasized that his party's main failing had been its lack of unity at critical times, exacerbated by 'Soviet interference and American irresolution'. But although these strictures showed how conscious Chiang was of his party's weaknesses and his enemy's strengths, he remained utterly convinced that the Guomindang was the only valid party for the Chinese nation. 'Our ideology, thought and political line are nevertheless definitely more correct than theirs and are moreover more suited to the needs of the nation.' That unwavering belief meant that nothing short of total victory was acceptable to him. It locked him into a struggle that became all or nothing. The result was that while, for expedient reasons, when things were going particularly badly for his forces, he appeared at times to be prepared to negotiate, in reality he was unwilling to settle for a genuine compromise.

Yet while the list of the military limitations of the Nationalists clearly goes a long way towards explaining their defeat, other factors were of considerable significance. A crippling political problem for Chiang Kai-shek was that his party never lived up to its own expectations. Sun Yatsen, the GMD's founder, had created it as a party of the people. That was the essence of its original appeal. However, although Chiang continued to assert that his was a truly popular revolutionary party, reality belied the claim. Famine was endemic in parts of China and although it is difficult to see how any government could have totally prevented it, the GMD's powerlessness in the face of its ravages further illustrated the emptiness of Chiang's claims that his government existed to end the poverty and hunger of the Chinese people.

Far from being a party of the people, the GMD under Chiang became a party of China's small social and financial elite. It drew its support from the bankers and merchants of urban China, who tended either to despise or to ignore the impoverished peasants of the countryside. The party depended on the donations and tax revenue that it drew from this numerically small but disproportionately influential class. A telling illustration of this was that 90 per cent of the revenue raised by the Nationalist government came from Shanghai, China's largest international port and money market.

The consequence was that the GMD government, reliant on deals with the shady elements in Chinese society, became essentially corrupt, gaining an unenviable but deserved reputation for nepotism and partiality. Such failings seemed all the more culpable in Nationalist China, since they contradicted the principles on which the GMD government was avowedly based. In 1943 Chiang had written a celebrated book, *China's Destiny*, in which he called upon the Chinese people to suppress all selfish thoughts and join with his party in a great national movement of moral regeneration. Such an appeal rang increasingly hollow as China slipped further into decline and the interests of the ordinary Chinese citizens were disregarded.

Of equal importance to corruption as a weakening factor for the Nationalists was their failure to cultivate a power base among the regional elites. Corrupt but effective governments can survive; corrupt but ineffective governments cannot. A problem that had confronted all leaders of China since the days of the emperors was the difficulty of imposing and maintaining central government on the regions of such a vast country. The common response was for central authorities to do a deal with local powers. In return for formal recognition of its overall authority, the central government would agree to leave the local magnates free to control regional affairs. It was a compromise that suited both sides and it broke down only when one of them declined to keep to the bargain.

Chiang Kai-shek's failure lay in his breach of this unwritten but established rule. By ignoring the traditional compromises, he offended the elites on whose co-operation his support ultimately depended. After 1945, when regaining the provinces which the Japanese had occupied, he tried to reimpose GMD control without sufficient thought for the local power structures. The professionals – businessmen, lawyers and financiers – who had stayed on to administer the regions during the Japanese war expected to keep their positions after the GMD's return to power. But Chiang, convinced that he could control things without reference to the actual political and social conditions in the provinces, chose to replace them with his own nominees. It was a mistake from which he never recovered.

Denied the loyalty that more understanding policies on his part might have encouraged among the local elites, Chiang was left with only one course of action – coercion. Unable to create a genuine following, he tried to enforce support by terror tactics. This occasionally brought acquiescence, but never real support. Chiang forfeited the goodwill of those sections of the population whose backing his regime most needed. Such failure played into the hands of Mao and the CCP.

A particular irony was that, for all its association with the moneyed interests of China, Chiang's government had a disastrous economic record. The Nationalists' 12 years in power after 1937 were dominated by the struggle against Japan and the Communists with the result that the bulk of the government's revenue was consumed in military expenditure. This effectively ended any possibility of significant investment in the domestic economy.

The financial policies the GMD was obliged to pursue in its attempt to remain solvent added to the distaste felt towards it. Besides imposing severe taxes on individuals and companies, the government nationalized China's private banks and finance houses. But since the revenue acquired by such means proved insufficient, the government still relied on loans from foreign financiers. Such indebtedness might have been acceptable, even if only grudgingly, to China's bankers had Chiang's government not fallen victim to one of its greatest wartime opponents – inflation.

Inflation in China, 1942–48		
Year	Notes issued (in millions of Chinese dollars)	Price index (100 in 1937)
1942	35,100	6,620
1943	75,400	22,800
1944	189,500	75,500
1945	1,031,900	249,100
1946	3,726,100	627,000
1947	33,188,500	10,340,000
1948	374,762,200	287,700,000

What became hyper-inflation progressively undermined Nationalist China, rendering it a currency speculator's paradise. A mixture of local currencies, sterling and American dollars meant that food prices had no consistent value and varied by as much as 300 per cent between one city and another. As the military situation became desperate from 1948 onwards, the Nationalists tried frantically to restore financial stability. In an attempt to control inflation, currency values were tied to gold. Strong-arm tactics were employed to force people to exchange their gold, silver and precious stones for a new paper currency, and a show was made of arresting and publicly shaming large-scale speculators. But a system built on deals with racketeers and profiteers could hardly hope to survive by attacking racketeering and profiteering. The currency was too damaged to recover and the newly issued banknotes plunged in value.

In many areas, money ceased to have any meaning, and barter became the norm. Rather than achieving

progress, China had returned to economic primitivism.
By 1949, financial collapse had led inexorably to social
disruption, which could be contained only by repression
of a ferocity reminiscent of the excesses perpetrated by
the warlords and the Japanese; all this undermined the
GMD's claim to bring liberty to the Chinese people.

Economic failure is seldom a sufficient factor in itself
to bring down a government. If a regime has enough
strength of purpose and military power, it can sustain itself.
In the end it was the loss of faith among key elements in
the GMD that weakened government and party resolve.
This decline in morale in turn affected the armed services
and prevented Chiang's forces from turning their initial
superiority into final victory. Ultimately it was the most
obvious of factors in war – military competence – that
produced the CCP's triumph in 1949.

Shanghai, November
1949 – with
food becoming
scarcer and more
expensive, people
scrabble for beans
and grains that
have dropped from
a passing truck.
(Bettmann/Getty
Images)

Mao described the CCP's victory as having come in three main stages: the CCP's success in holding on to Manchuria, the defeat of the GMD's 'strongpoint offensive' in 1947–48, and the PLA's counter-offensives in 1948–49. The received version of events in Communist China after Mao had come to power was that he had followed a carefully planned path to victory. Never depending on the USSR for support, and overcoming the hostile interference of the imperialist Americans, he had had the courage and wisdom to strike out on his own. Knowing that the people were the ultimate source of power, he had aroused them in a great crusade against the GMD. The land reforms that had been implemented by the Communists in the liberated areas had shown both the organizing abilities and the generosity of spirit of the CCP. That is why the people had flocked to the Communists' cause, eager recruits more than trebling the size of Mao's armies and making them an unstoppable force that, under Mao's inspired direction, drove the Nationalists from the mainland.

There were elements of truth in this story but much of it was distortion. Mao's genius lay in his opportunism rather than his long-term planning. At the start of the Civil War, his essential aim was to survive by consolidating in those areas where the CCP had bases. He could not foresee that within three years he would be master of mainland China. It was Chiang's strategic mistakes and political and economic failures that made that possible. The Communists, it has to be added, also suffered from serious defects, which, had the GMD been able to exploit them, might have changed the outcome of the war. The CCP's land reform policy may have brought some justice to the countryside by ending landlord exploitation, but its chief purpose was to provide a mechanism for the fierce enforcement of Communist political and social control. Contrary to the CCP's propaganda claim that it was the support of the liberated Chinese peasants that won the war, it is notable that there were few genuine and sustained popular risings in support of the Communists. Fear was a far more potent factor in bringing recruits to the Communist cause than committed enthusiasm. Chiang's tragedy was that he could not turn this fear to his advantage since his own regime was equally repressive.

A vital element in Mao's triumph was the strength of the political power he had come to exercise within the CCP by 1945. The determination with which he prosecuted the Civil War once the PLA had gone on the offensive was of a piece with the ruthlessness he had shown in establishing his authority over the CCP. Historians now emphasize his abilities as a military leader and suggest that chief among the factors accounting for the CCP's ultimate victory was Mao's generalship. It was under him that the Communist forces, who were essentially rural guerrilla fighters in 1945, had, by 1949, become a modern army capable of conducting a modern war. The most compelling example of this was Mao's willingness to press on with the three massive campaigns of the winter of 1948/49. This was warfare on a scale never previously seen in China. Indeed, such was the scale of the campaigns that some of Mao's commanders doubted that they could be fought successfully. That Mao was able to overcome these doubts and drive his armies on to a series of decisive victories that won the war for the CCP illustrates his power of command, and his burning belief in his own judgement.

Of major significance in the ultimate Civil War victory of Mao's Communists was that the conflict more often took the form not of pitched battles but of sieges, the greater number laid by the PLA. Siege warfare worked greatly to the Communists' advantage. It is a striking psychological phenomenon that in a protracted siege it is often the political and military leaders in the besieged region who become more hated, since it is they who have to impose increasingly severe restrictions on food supply and movement. It is common for suffering inhabitants who are not ideologically committed but simply trying to survive to come to regard the attacking forces when successful as bringing liberation. The CCP took great advantage of this, encouraging desperate

A PLA soldier in 1950, carrying a US-made Johnson automatic rifle, one of the huge number of American weapons originally supplied to the Nationalist armies but captured and used by the Communists. (Philip Jowett)

starving people to escape and come over to them. It was such developments that gave strength to the Communists' claim that they were the true liberators of the Chinese people. Of course, there were occasions, as at Changchun, when the PLA treated the civilian survivors of a siege with great brutality, but this did not prevent the Communists from winning the propaganda war on a larger front.

CONCLUSION AND CONSEQUENCES
The legacy of the Civil War

Figures of the number of deaths resulting from the Chinese Civil War are imprecise, but all estimates suggest that the carnage was appalling. In the three major campaigns that decided the war, the Nationalists lost over one and a half million men, the Communists approaching a quarter of a million. That total can be doubled for the war overall; some commentators have put the figure as high as six million. This total includes the Chinese civilians who died from the famine and disruption that accompanied the war or who were the victims of the terror tactics used deliberately by both sides.

It was not the death toll alone that made the legacy of the Civil War a bitter one. The struggle enthroned authoritarianism, deified Mao as a supremely wise leader whose word was law, justified fierce 'anti' campaigns against those judged to be dissidents, and made mass mobilization of the peasantry a basic means of social action. It enshrined Marxism-Leninism not because of its quality as a political theory, but because its dogmatism perfectly suited and complemented the traditional Chinese notion that the people's duty was to obey those in power.

The Civil War had not been a struggle about principle and ideology, though that was often the language in which it was couched. Instead, it had been a naked struggle for military supremacy. Having achieved power by breaking its military and political adversaries, the CCP under Mao proceeded to establish a new Chinese state whose hallmarks were its readiness to coerce its people into line and to destroy those who opposed its rule. The guiding concept to which Mao adhered was that politics, like war, was a constant conflict. In that regard it was a continuation of the dialectical pattern of Chinese thought. His oft-quoted utterance that 'all power grows out of the barrel of a gun' was for him to be as much a truism in peacetime as it had been in war.

The Chinese Civil War was much more than a parenthesis to the larger Cold War. Indeed, what happened in China between 1946 and 1949 helped shape the Cold War. It is legitimate to speculate that without Mao's victory in 1949, the United States would not have developed its aggressive response to what it saw as the creation of a Sino-Soviet Communist monolith. The Soviet Union without China as an ideological ally would have had to be far more circumspect in its approach to international relations, with the result that hostility between East and West would not have intensified in the way that it did. Had China not gone Communist in 1949, there would have been no Korean War in 1950 and no Vietnam War in the 1960s.

However, important though Mao's victory was in Cold War terms, its significance goes further. Viewed from an Eastern perspective, the Chinese struggle was of huge consequence to Asia. It led to the creation of modern China – a nation structured on the basis of not only a rejection of many Western values, but also a rejection of Communist ones as represented by the Soviet Union. There is also a sense in which the Civil War freed China to follow its own path, which is what Mao meant when in 1949 he declared that 'China has stood up.' Achieved in the face of both American and Soviet opposition, the Communist victory over the Nationalists marked a formative stage in the rise of China as a world power, seemingly destined to become the most influential force in international affairs in the 21st century.

Mao is perhaps best remembered in history as an extraordinary political figure who, after 1949, recreated China as a nation in his own image. But it must not be forgotten that his control of China was a product of his success in the field. His political ideas were obviously of intrinsic importance, but they would have counted for little had he not won the war. And ideology does not win wars unless it can be translated into realistic and practical action.

A triumphant Mao Zedong surveys a parade of captured GMD anti-aircraft guns, Beijing, 1949. (Photo by Keystone-France/Gamma-Keystone via Getty Images)

The legacy for the victorious CCP was the belief that the methods and strategy that had won the Civil War applied also to the politics of peacetime. It was the memory of the military victories achieved between 1946 and 1949 that inspired Mao's adoption of coercion as the principal means of running the new China that he had brought into being.

Yet a final irony intrudes. China became a great power not because of Mao but in spite of him. For all his ability to create a nation dedicated to a political ideal, the power of China in the 21st century rests not on its politics but its economics. There is a sense in which Chiang Kai-shek proved the final victor. He and his successors' development of Taiwan as one of the 'tiger economies' of the second half of the 20th century became the unacknowledged capitalist model on which Mao's successors, abandoning his dated policies, began to build modern China.

There is also a sense in which the Chinese Civil War has not ended; no formal peace treaty or agreement has ever been made. The conflict that began in the era of the Cold War has outlived that larger struggle. The two Chinese states that emerged from the Civil War, the PRC and Taiwan, have followed very different paths in their subsequent development, but each side continues to claim that it alone is the legitimate government of the whole of China. In the third decade of the 21st century, the issues over which the Civil War had been fought three quarters of a century earlier have still to be resolved. Xi Jinping, PRC leader since 2012, has repeatedly declared the right of the PRC to reclaim Taiwan for the mainland, by military means if necessary.

This monument in Lhasa, Tibet's capital, depicts Mao Zedong and his successors: Deng Xiaoping, Jiang Zemin, Hu Jintao and Xi Jinping. Xi's wish to present himself as a successor to Mao has particular relevance to the PRC's claim to Taiwan. (Photo by Roman Balandin\ TASS via Getty Images)

APPENDIX & CHRONOLOGY

Appendix: Military Commanders

PLA

Chen Yi	Commander of the East China Field Army
Deng Xiaoping	Organised the taking of Xuzhou and Suxian and the crossing of the Yangzi
He Long	A principal organiser of PLA strategy in Manchuria and northern China
Lin Biao	Commander-in-chief of the Manchurian Field Army. He led the taking of Harbin and Jinzhou and played a key role in the Liaoshen and Pingjin campaigns
Liu Bocheng	Commander of the Central Plains Army
Nie Rongzhen	Led resistance to the NRA's strongpoint campaign and was a co-commander of the Pingjin campaign
Peng Dehuai	Commander of the PLA's northwest field army
Su Yu	Was entrusted with the main planning of the Huaihai campaign
Zhang Zhenglong	A PLA colonel, he was an eyewitness to the Changchun massacre

NRA

Chen Changjie	Commander who surrendered Tianjin to the PLA
Du Yuming	Chiang loyalist commander who lost Xuzhou
Fu Zuoyi	Unsuccessful defender of Beijing
Guo Jingyun	Commander in Xinbaoan who shot himself after its fall to the PLA
Hu Zongnan	Successfully took a deserted Yanan in what proved to be an empty victory, since he had already leaked details of his intended moves to the Communists
Huang Baitao	General of the 7th Army Group. He committed suicide after losing Xuzhou and Zhanzhuan
Li Zongren	Took over as GMD leader after Chiang gave up defending the mainland in 1949
Liao Yaoxiang	Commander of the NRA New 1st Army and defender of Shenyang, which ultimately proved futile
Liu Zhih	Commander who was defeated at Xuzhou,

	which led to the fall of Nanjing
Tang Enbo	Fanatical and murderous governor of Shanghai
Qiu Qinquan	The 2nd NRA Army commander whose reluctance to fight led to the fall of Xuzhou
Wei Lihuang	Chiang's commander-in-chief in the north-east
Zheng Dongguao	Gallant commander and defender of Changchun, but finally overburdened
Zhou Fucheng	Inherited from Wei Lihuang the impossible task of saving Shenyang

Chronology

1945

4–11 February	Yalta Conference
6 and 9 August	Atomic bombing of Hiroshima and Nagasaki
14 August	Sino-Soviet Treaty of Friendship
28 August	Mao flies with Hurley to Chongqing for start of CCP–GMD talks, meets Chiang for the first time in 20 years
2 September	Formal Japanese surrender
11 October	Mao returns to Yanan from Chongqing
21 December	Start of Marshall mission to China

1946

May	Soviet forces leave Manchuria. PLA take Harbin
10 June	Short-lived ceasefire in Manchuria
26 June	Civil War starts
December	Start of NRA counter-attacks

1947

7 January	End of Marshall mission
January–March	NRA takes over 150 towns
28 February	Demonstrations in Taiwan against GMD takeover
March	NRA repulsed by Lin Biao's forces at Harbin
19 March	Nationalists take Yanan
May–December	Unsuccessful NRA 'strongpoint offensive'
7 August	Chiang visits Yanan

1948

May	Mao establishes his military HQ at Xibaipo in Hebei province
12 September	Start of Liaoshen campaign
15 October	GMD surrenders Jinzhou
20–28 October	Battle of Liaoxi
26 October	Changchun surrenders to PLA
2 November	Fall of Shenyang to PLA
6 November	Start of Huaihai campaign
12 November	Liaoshen campaign ends in NRA defeat
22 November	NRA 7th Army capitulates at Zhanzhuan
29 November	Start of Pingjin campaign
22 December	Fall of Xinbaoan to PLA
23 December	PLA takes Zhangjiakou

1949

10 January	Xuzhou falls to PLA; Huaihai campaign ends in NRA defeat
15 January	Fall of Tianjin to PLA
16 January	Beijing surrenders to PLA without a fight
21 January	Chiang Kai-shek passes presidency of GMD to Li Zongren
31 January	Triumphal entry of PLA into Beijing; end of Pingjin campaign
20 April	PLA crosses the Yangzi; British ship HMS *Amethyst* fired on in Yangzi
23 April	Fall of Nanjing to PLA
20 May	NRA surrenders Xian
24 May	Fall of Shanghai to PLA
July	HMS *Amethyst* sails down Yangzi to safety
22 August	NRA surrenders Changsha to PLA
10 September	Mao takes up residence in Beijing
1 October	Mao proclaims creation of PRC
28 October	Ghangzhou falls to PLA
1 December	Fall of Chongqing to PLA
10 December	Chiang Kai-shek's flight to Taiwan, as he leaves mainland China for the last time

FURTHER READING

Belden, Jack, *China Shakes the World*, Harper & Brothers, New York (1949)

Chang, Jung and Halliday, Jon, *Mao: The Unknown Story*, Vintage, London (2006)

Chassin, Lionel, *The Communist Conquest of China: A History of the Civil War*, Harvard University Press, Cambridge (1965)

Dikötter, Frank, *The Age of Openness: China before Mao*, Hong Kong University Press, Hong Kong (2014)

Dikötter, Frank, *The Tragedy of Liberation: A History of the Chinese Revolution 1945–57*, Bloomsbury Publishing, London (2016)

Dillon, Michael, *China: A Modern History*, I.B. Tauris, London (2012)

Dillon, Michael (Ed), *Encyclopedia of Chinese History*, Routledge, Abingdon (2017)

Dillon, Michael, *Zhou Enlai: The Enigma Behind Chairman Mao*, I.B. Tauris, London (2018)

Fenby, Jonathan, *Generalissimo Chiang Kai-shek and the World He Lost*, Free Press, London (2003)

Fenby, Jonathan, *The Penguin History of Modern China: The Fall and Rise of a Great Power, 1850–2008*, Penguin, London (2008)

Gray, Jack, *Rebellions and Revolutions: China from the 1800s to 2000*, Oxford University Press, Oxford (2002)

Lary, Diana, *China's Civil War: A Social History, 1945–49*, Cambridge University Press, Cambridge (2015)

Levine, Steven, *Anvil of Victory: The Communist Revolution in Manchuria, 1945–1948*, Columbia University Press, New York (1987)

Lew, Christopher, *The Third Chinese Revolutionary Civil War, 1945–49*, Routledge, Abingdon (2009)

Lynch, Michael, *Mao*, Routledge, Abingdon (2017)

Lynch, Michael, *Modern China*, Hodder Headline, London (2006)

May, Ernest, *The Truman Administration in China, 1945–1949*, Lippincott, New York (1975)

Melby, John, *The Mandate of Heaven, Record of a Civil War: China 1945–1949*, University of Toronto Press, Toronto (1968)

Mitter, Rana, *A Bitter Revolution: China's Struggle with the Modern World*, Oxford University Press, Oxford (2004)

Pepper, Suzanne, *Civil War in China: The Political Struggle, 1945–1949*, University of California Press, Berkeley (1978)

Pogue, Forrest, *George C. Marshall: Statesman, 1945–1959*, Viking Press, New York (1987)

Shun-hsin, Chou, *The Chinese Inflation, 1937–1949*, Columbia University Press, New York (1963)

Spence, Jonathan, *The Search for Modern China*, W. W. Norton, London (2013)

Tsou Tang, *America's Failure in China, 1941–1950*, University of Chicago Press, Chicago (1989)

Westad, Odd Arne, *Decisive Encounters: The Chinese Civil War, 1946–1950*, Stanford University Press, Stanford (2003)

Xiaobing Li, *A History of the Modern Chinese Army*, University Press of Kentucky, Kentucky (2007)

INDEX